© 2024 by Brandon Publishing

All rights reserved. No portion of this book may be reproduced, stored in a retrieval system, or transmitted in any form or by any means—electronic, mechanical, photocopy, recording, scanning, or other—except for brief quotations in critical reviews or articles, without the prior written permission of the publisher or The University of Michigan Flint's KCP Program.

Interior Design by Brandon Publishing

Project Interior Edits by: Aniya Loren Callaway

Brandon Publishing titles may be purchased in bulk for educational, business, fundraising, or sales promotional use. For information, please email orderimpact@gmail.com

ISBN: 9798309349586

Printed in the United States of America
15 16 17 18 19 RRD 6 5 4 3 2 1

Harmony of Expression

An Anthology Of Creativity & Writing

Table of Contents

Author	Page
Introduction	11
Zayadi	13
Wills	15
Webster	19
Anonymous	21
Anonymous	25
Trzil	29
Smith	33
Smith	37
Simon	41
Sabadac	43
Rudy	47
Robinson	51
Rivers	53
Randolph	55
Anonymous	59

Table of Contents

Author	Page
Trzil	61
Powell	65
Palmer	71
Ouedraogo	75
Numan	79
Moore	83
Modrak	87
McQuiller	89
Malone	93
Maldonado	97
Kirks	101
Jones	117
Johnson	121
Johnson	125
James	129
Ivanac	141
Hartman	145
Anonymous	149

Table of Contents

Author	Page
Garrett	163
Franz	165
Fischer	169
Doss	173
Docherty	177
Anonymous	181
Cusac	183
Conner	185
Collins	189
Colin	193
Anonymous	195
Choice	199
Callaway	201
Anonymous	205
Brown	207
Bishai	211
Christian	215
Barginere-Claxton	219

Table of Contents

Author	Page
Baird	*221*
Anonymous	*223*
Al-Shawi	*225*
Anonymous	*231*

Introduction

The King-Chavez-Parks Program welcomes readers to "Harmony of Expression: An Anthology of Creativity, Art, and Writing." This exceptional collection is a testament to the creativity and passion that flourishes within the minds of scholars at the University of Michigan-Flint. Within these pages, you will find a diverse array of works, including poignant essays that delve into personal stories, evocative poetry that captures the essence of human experience, and stunning visual art that reflects the unique perspectives of our students.

Each piece in this anthology is a window into the hearts and minds of the contributors, offering insights into their moments of need, life lessons that have shaped them, and the myriad experiences that define their journeys. Through their art and writing, these students express themselves and connect with readers on a profound level, sharing universal themes of struggle, triumph, and discovery.

The King-Chavez-Parks Program, a grant-funded initiative at the University of Michigan-Flint, is dedicated to fostering a supportive and engaging environment for students. By providing comprehensive academic support and enrichment opportunities, the program empowers students to achieve their full potential. Open and free to all enrolled students, the King Chavez Parks Program embodies a commitment to inclusivity and excellence, ensuring that every student has the resources and encouragement they need to succeed.

KCP
What It Means To Me
by Miriam Zayadi

Zayadi

With a daunting yet hopeful new start, it is from our family's homes we depart

With the purpose of chasing distant dreams, overwhelming and impossible it all seems

With guiding arms pulling us from the dark, we find refuge in King-Chavez-Parks

With not only housing, mentorship, and financial aid, but lifelong connections that are made

You have shown us the way to our true path, offering tutoring in English, science, and math

You host events that teach us to network, not to mention the stipends are a major perk

You, who carries the legacy of three great names, ignite our passions and fan the flames

You who kept us from trying to quit, showed us the meaning of having true grit

Always will benefit from the KCP honor
Always will remember my time as a Promise Scholar

My Journey As A Student During The COVID-19 Pandemic

by Naomi Wills

Harmony of Expressions

Despite the challenges presented by the COVID-19 pandemic, my experience as an online student has prepared me for success in my senior year of college, as I am back on campus and on track to graduate.

The unexpected start of the COVID-19 pandemic dramatically changed the educational world, causing students to deal with a lot of change and adjust suddenly. I was one of those students. I had to start my college journey with online classes. At the time, nobody was sure how well online classes could replace in-person classes. I had to find out if I was academically and personally prepared to face this change.

The shift from in-person to online classes tested my academic resolve and personal resilience. As I worked my way through taking exams online and attending virtual classes, these attributes enabled me to overcome the challenges an online learning environment poses.

Now, as I step back onto campus in my senior year and see graduation in the not-so-distant future, I'm fully aware of the impact that juggling my various experiences has had on my growth as a person and a student. Embracing adaptability and stimulating determination were significant in successfully managing the shift to online learning during the pandemic and continue influencing my final year on campus.

Returning to campus has brought a smooth transition and a deeper understanding of academic involvement. Skills such as self-discipline, proactive communication, and technological proficiency—have become invaluable as I navigate this final chapter of my college education. This situation has not only prepared me to tackle academic challenges with renewed vigor but also allowed me to contribute meaningfully to campus life, participating in discussions and projects with a deeper appreciation for collaborative learning.

I know for myself it was difficult to start college virtually, so I am glad to hear others made it through that period and are graduating this year. As I approach graduation, it is evident that the adversity I faced during those initial online semesters was not an impediment but rather an opportunity for growth in overcoming even the most unforeseen challenges.

In conclusion, transitioning from in-person classes to online learning during the COVID-19 pandemic was not just a temporary academic hurdle but a transformative experience that profoundly impacted my personal and educational growth. Learning to eliminate procrastination and encourage time management contributed to making it through the changes the pandemic brought. These qualities did not merely assist me in managing the immediate challenges of virtual education; they have become integral components of my approach to learning and facing life's uncertainties.

As I continue my final year on campus, the lessons learned during those initial days of the pandemic remain ever-relevant. They remind me

Harmony of Expressions

of the importance of resilience in both academic pursuits and personal endeavors. My advice for future graduates is to keep going, and eventually, you will meet your goal. Looking ahead, these experiences will undoubtedly serve as a foundation for future challenges, ensuring that adaptability and determination remain at the forefront as I prepare to step into post-graduation with a world fraught with its own set of unknowns and opportunities.

Small Cabin
Tashala Webster

Harmony of Expressions

A small black rectangular box in the midst of trees
Wooden chairs near the fire pit,
where I watch the flames dance about as I sit
Surrounded by the beauty of animals roaming free
A true definition of peace and tranquility
As the outside world slowly disappears from me
I found my peace in a small cabin in the woods
With the sweet breeze and autumn leaves
Somewhere for me to be free
It is no better place to be
As the nature sings to me
Here is where I can reconnect with myself
Mentally and spiritually

A Poem
by Anonymous Writer

Harmony of Expressions

Blossoming into the next
As the sunlight hits my soil filled flesh, it's warm.
This warmth fills my heart and soul with courage.

My tear filled rain slowly drips off my petals and
onto the ground, maintaining a solid flow.
It grows. It grows. It grows.

Thorns emerge from my fingertips, cutting the
thread which connects me to outside the roots of my
mind.

Collect the loose strings and weave them together
Connecting each loose end and growing further out
into the world

Unfamiliar soil, unfamiliar terrain.
Unable to yet blossom, I wonder
Could the outside soil maintain my growth?

With the string I've collected I throw my seeds out
into the open ground.
It grows. It grows. It grows

Sudden death from one plant, emerges the next
blossoming
The nectar from my stems grows into something
sweet and tender

Harmony of Expressions

Spewing sweetness, from the heart I become new
How to refuse?
When the blossom I've become, is made into the one which fuels you.

Tender love and care is all one needs,
For as the flower blooms,
Balance filled love arrives within you.

A Personal Essay
Anonymous

Harmony of Expressions

Growing up in Flint, Michigan, I faced many challenges that profoundly impacted my self-worth and belonging. Social acceptance was difficult to achieve, and I struggled to connect with others, which made me feel emotionally isolated. As a young woman, I had social anxiety and constantly sought approval from my peers, which only made my anxiety worse over time. Coping with a learning disability in elementary school also complicated my academic and social experiences, despite the support of my father, who sometimes said things that unintentionally made me doubt myself.

To compensate for my insecurities, I often talked excessively in social settings, fearing rejection due to my eagerness to connect. This behavior made my anxiety worse and contributed to the development of body dysmorphia and heightened concerns about my weight, adding layers of complexity to my journey toward self-acceptance.

As I navigated through adolescence and early adulthood, I gradually recognized the profound impact of these challenges on my self-image and confidence. During this period, I decided to seek professional help and prioritize self-care. This journey toward self-acceptance was gradual yet transformative. Therapy became a cornerstone in managing my social anxiety and body dysmorphia, fostering introspection and self-compassion. Through therapy, I realized that self-acceptance does not depend on external validation but on embracing my uniqueness and acknowledging my strengths, particularly my resilience and determination.

Harmony of Expressions

The absence of a maternal figure significantly influenced my struggle with belonging and anxiety during my transition into adulthood. Without a mother's guidance and nurturing presence, I often felt a deep void and heightened insecurity, amplifying my quest for approval and connection in social settings. I usually thought that there was something wrong with me.

Despite these challenges, I gradually learned to embrace my unique path and recognize the strength of overcoming adversity independently. Through self-discovery and seeking professional support, I cultivated self-compassion and gained a deeper understanding of my intrinsic worth.

Reflecting on my journey, I acknowledge the importance of connecting with supportive figures and communities. While my upbringing presented hurdles, it ultimately fueled my commitment to fostering a sense of belonging and acceptance within myself and the broader community.

Today, I carry forward these lessons by advocating for self-acceptance and empathy and encouraging others to embrace their journeys with resilience and compassion. By sharing my experiences, I aim to inspire individuals facing similar challenges to recognize their inner strength and capacity for growth, fostering a community where everyone feels valued and supported on their path to self-acceptance and fulfillment. Self-acceptance is not merely a destination but a transformative journey toward personal empowerment and communal acceptance as a student.

A Personal Essay

Elijah Trzil

Harmony of Expressions

Growing up, I endured the pain and humiliation of physical bullying. Each day at school was marked by taunts, threats, and violence that left me feeling helpless and afraid. It seemed like there was no escape from pain, until I discovered the life-changing power of martial arts.

Joining martial arts was a turning point in my life. Stepping into the dojo for the first time, I was welcomed into a community of like-minded individuals who shared a passion for discipline, respect, and self-improvement. Here, I found not only a means of defending myself but also a path to personal growth and empowerment. Martial arts taught me a set of valuable skills that transcended mere physical combat. Yes, I learned to defend myself with speed and precision, mastering techniques that allowed me to protect myself from harm. But more importantly, I learned the importance of discipline and perseverance in the face of adversity. Through intense training and unwavering dedication, I honed my physical abilities and mental fortitude. I discovered the strength that comes from pushing past my limits and embracing discomfort. Each session in the dojo was a lesson in resilience, teaching me to never give up, no matter how daunting the challenge.

Perhaps the most profound lesson martial arts taught me was the value of respect and humility. In the dojo, ego had no place, and students were expected to treat each other with kindness and dignity. Through sparring and training alongside my peers, I learned to set aside differences and work together towards a common goal. I gained a newfound appre-

ciation for the strength that comes from unity and cooperation, realizing that we are all stronger when we lift each other up. Martial arts also taught me the importance of focus and mindfulness. Through meditation and breathing exercises, I learned to quiet my mind and stay present in the moment.
This newfound mental clarity not only enhanced my performance in training but also poured over into other areas of my life. I became more focused and disciplined in my studies and more resilient in the face of challenges. Beyond the physical and mental benefits, martial arts provided me with a sense of purpose and belonging. In the dojo, I found a second family, a supportive community of individuals who uplifted and encouraged me every step of the way. Together, we shared triumphs and setbacks, pushing each other to be the best versions of ourselves.

In conclusion, my journey through martial arts has been a testament to the transformative power of perseverance, discipline, and self-discovery. What began as a means of self-defense evolved into a lifelong passion, shaping me into the confident and resilient individual I am today. Through martial arts, I not only learned to defend myself but also discovered the strength within myself to overcome any obstacle life throws my way.

Summer Of Opportunity

Summer Smith

Harmony of Expressions

It all started at the end of my senior year of high school. I had been trying to find my college. I was offered to participate in the Promise Scholar Program, which sealed the deal for me to go to the University of Michigan—Flint. My mom and I both felt it would not only offer me many opportunities but also be close to home and cost-effective. It would be the start of my college journey.

With the program came the starting opportunity to do two college classes in the summer with room and board. My mother felt this was an incredible opportunity for me. I felt that it was not so much. This was taking away from my "senior summer" before college. I always had this vision for the last summer after high school, something out of a high school musical. It would be the perfect summer to go to the beach, hang out with friends, and go shopping. All the movie's perfect events. However, my mom felt I should start college early and join the summer bridge program.

I struggled to decide what to do with my summer, and so many choices existed. My mom wants me to go to college, and I would like to have a fun summer or even a gap year. That idea was absolutely off the table among many people in my family. So that was not going to happen. One thing I did know is that I wanted to get out of the house as soon as possible. As graduation came near, the obligation faded as I got older. There were a lot of bumping heads at this time. I weighed out the pros and cons of going to Summer Bridge. I decided it couldn't be too bad to start college early.

That ended up being one of the best decisions I could have made. I am eternally grateful to my mom. She got me to take advantage of this great opportunity I did not realize then. In the summer, I experienced many unique opportunities. It truly changed my life, my view of college, and so many other aspects.

That summer, I learned so many different things, including many staff members on campus, students, and, best of all, campus. I got a really good feeling about campus. I could envision myself here; it was my new home. I got to explore campus and Flint during the summer. This helped me feel comfortable when starting in the fall. I had one up on the other freshman coming in the fall. Taking college classes in the summer also allowed me to see how these classes run and helped me manage my time to get everything done before the due dates. I learned to block my time and keep track of important dates and reminders on a calendar. These were valuable skills to have in college.

I came into the fall semester knowing how to find resources on campus, such as booking a study room in the library. I feel this is something that if you don't get told how to do, you may not know. So, regarding midterms, I knew you could book ahead of time, something not all students may learn. Along with just lovely places to hang out on campus, this knowledge of campus helped me help other students and even get my job as an orientation leader.

The transformative impact of the summer bridge program on my sense of belonging and perspective

Harmony of Expressions

on college has been profound. It has provided me with a supportive community and equipped me with invaluable skills and insights that have reshaped my approach to learning and personal growth. Through this program, I have learned the importance of perseverance, collaboration, and embracing new challenges with an open mind. It has ignited a passion to make the most of my college experience and actively contribute to my academic and personal development. I am grateful for the opportunities and experiences the program has offered me, and I am excited to continue my college journey with a newfound sense of purpose and enthusiasm.

Personal Experiences

Rayonna Smith

Harmony of Expressions

The impact of Covid-19 on my high school senior year was profound and deeply disappointing. Amidst the excitement of nearing graduation, I found myself unable to participate in any senior activities, including the much-anticipated prom. This absence left me yearning for those cherished experiences I had looked forward to for so long.

One of the most disheartening aspects was the inability to bid farewell or extend congratulations to my classmates properly. The sudden disruption of our final year together left a palpable void, denying us the closure we deserved after years of shared experiences. The onset of Covid-19 ushered in a period of profound boredom and isolation. The stringent safety measures necessitated staying indoors, resulting in a stark separation from loved ones and the outside world. Fear of the virus's potential consequences loomed large, further restricting social interactions and outings.

Witnessing the toll of the virus firsthand, with numerous acquaintances falling ill, underscored the gravity of the situation. It served as a stark reminder of the importance of rigorous hand hygiene and overall vigilance in mitigating the spread of infectious diseases. Even as time has passed, the impact of Covid-19 continues to reverberate within our communities. The recent loss of a family member to the virus served as a stark reminder of its enduring threat. The absence of prom due to the Covid-19 virus was a devastating blow after meticulously planning and eagerly anticipating the event.

Instead of the vibrant celebration I had envisioned, I found myself relegated to a drive-thru open house—a stark contrast to the joyous gathering I had hoped for. The inability to gather with friends and family for my graduation party compounded the disappointment. I longed to share in the festivities and bask in the camaraderie of my loved ones, yet the circumstances imposed by the pandemic thwarted those aspirations. Moreover, the absence of a traditional graduation ceremony deprived me of the opportunity to express my gratitude to the teachers who had profoundly impacted my life. Throughout the years, they had imparted invaluable wisdom and guidance, shaping me into the person I had become. Covid-19 not only deprived me of cherished memories but also tainted what should have been a momentous occasion with negativity and regret. Instead of commemorating my achievements with joy and pride, I found myself mired in disappointment and longing for what could have been.

Reflecting on my senior year, it's evident that the virus cast a long shadow over what should have been a milestone period in my life. Its disruptive force not only robbed me of cherished experiences but also imparted valuable lessons about resilience, empathy, and the fragility of human life. Despite the challenges it presented, I emerged from this ordeal with a newfound appreciation for the importance of human connection and the resilience of the human spirit.

Journey Of Healing

Grace Simon

Harmony of Expressions

In shattered silence, echoes weep,
As wounded hearts begin to creep.
Through tears that fall like morning dew,
A journey starts, a path to pursue.
In broken fragments, pain resides,
Yet healing whispers through the tides.
With each sunrise, a gentle balm,
To mend the wounds, to bring calm.
Through time's embrace, the ache may fade,
As memories soften in the shade.
Though scars remain, they tell a story,
Of strength reclaimed, of new found glory.
In heartbreak's wake, resilience thrives,
As broken hearts learn to revive.
For in the depths of sorrow's flight,
Healing blooms, in quiet light.

My Life Experience During The Covid-19 Pandemic

Matthew Sabadac

Harmony of Expressions

It seems like yesterday; it has been a while, in fact, it has been more than four years. For some, the pandemic time may seem like a lifetime ago; for others, they may seem as recent as yesterday, but it is indisputable that Covid has changed the lives and the world of all of us.

When I think back to the pandemic time, what do I remember? We have now entered the fifth year since the World Health Organization declared Covid-19 as a global pandemic on March 11, 2020, after our normality has been altered, and normal life has ceased to exist. In the beginning, I thought this might only be something temporary, and like me, many others thought the same. But no, it was not like that, it appears that things will never return to normal. I remember that each time we started to see a light at the end of the tunnel, something unexpected happened, and more and more cases of Covid were being reported every single day.

What impact has it had on me, and my family? I was a junior in high school at the time of the outbreak of the pandemic. I will never forget that Friday, March 13th, when the entire high school was sent home, when we were told that virtual learning would begin on Monday, March 16th. Furthermore, they informed us that the goal was to end that year virtually, with the hope that in the fall we would be able to go back to school in person. Even though it's hard to believe, we were able to do that then, to go back to school in person, to attend "normal school". The school district where I studied was one of the two school districts of the 28 districts in Oakland

County that offered in person instruction all year. I was lucky, if I can say that because that was my senior year. It was very hard for us, for the students, for the teachers, for the parents, and for everybody else, to go in person to school in the pandemic time. Wasn't easy, lots of hard work, lots of stress, and lots of discipline too. Reflecting on my experiences as a virtual learner, I realized the most significant lesson learned was that I need to be very organized if I am to succeed, and also that I am more efficient when I complete a single task at a time, which is important because I previously opposed daily routines. Now, I strongly believe that having daily routines helped me.

During Covid I heard a few family friends complaining about how difficult the virtual learning system was from their young children who were in elementary or middle school. I helped some of them, it wasn't easy because I had to do it virtually, but now I understand how important it was that I was able to teach those kids, how to navigate virtually, how to keep up with the classes, and how to make it through those tough times. It was also important for me, because I managed to get through that period much more easily.

What lessons did I learn about myself and the world?

In conclusion, now more than four years later, I am thankful that I am healthy, thankful that everyone in my family was safe, thankful that we are together and why not thankful that we are stronger. Covid taught me how important it is to spend time

Harmony of Expressions

with my family, and how important it is to give back. Also, my attitude toward gratitude has changed significantly over these four years, and every little miracle that occurs around me makes me realize just how precious life is. The Covid-19 Pandemic experience has humbled me as a human being, and as a result there is a greater sense of empathy and compassion in me towards everyone.

The Village

Kaylee Rudy

Harmony of Expressions

A village is defined as "a small settlement usually found in a rural setting" by National Geographic. But my definition is a little different. To me, a village is a group of people who rally together to support somebody in any way possible. As someone who grew up with a single mom, I grew up in a large village. This village included many of my mom's friends, who quickly became my aunts, grandparents, aunts and uncles, and my extended family members. I can never remember a time when I felt entirely alone, because my village was always around.

A time when most people would feel alone would be when they are seriously injured. But for me, that wasn't the case. In February of 2023, I fell and broke my leg in 3 places. This in turn caused me to have 2 surgeries and 2 and a half months of physical therapy. But from February until May I was unable to leave the house without assistance. So this whole time, you would assume I was very alone, but I wasn't. I realized my village is large and so supportive. I was never left alone, someone was always home with me to take care of me. I also was receiving endless texts and calls from my friends and family making sure I was okay and also just making sure I felt included in life. When you are so secluded from the world while dealing with an injury, it is easy to fall into depression but my village made sure that wouldn't happen.

Another time when most children would have struggled would have been when adjusting to the transition from high school to college. My mom is

Rudy

my superhero, but she can't do everything alone. My family and friends gathered around me to be sure I had the most wonderful open house. My Aunt and Uncle came to help decorate and set up. The rest of my village came with arms full of gifts and words of encouragement.

When moving to college, I quickly learned my village was not only my hometown friends and family but also now my college friends. About two months into college, my grandpa abruptly passed away. He was one of my biggest supporters and one of my best friends. So losing him was hard. But my friends and teachers at school rallied around me to help in any way possible. My friends left sympathy gifts, waiting for me to come back to the dorms. My teachers gave me many extensions, and also their deepest sympathies. Also, the KCP program was quick to offer me support. Ms. Bianca and I met pretty regularly after my grandpa's death, she was someone easy to talk to, and encouraged me after that through anything I came to her with!

Through all these examples, you can see that I could have easily fallen off the straight and narrow path and made some mistakes. But with the help of my village, they kept me on the path to becoming the person I am today. My biggest advice to anyone young or old, is to build your village. Not only that but make sure people in your life, feel as if you are part of their village as well.

Love & Attention

Reese Robinson

Harmony of Expressions

love and attention

aren't they the same thing,
i never really thought so.

not when i was little and missing my front teeth.
back then i thought love was what falling asleep in
the car on a sunny day felt like.
or getting a bandaid to stick to my knee so i could
keep playing with my friends.

now that im older, and have all my teeth, love feels
like time passing by.
time spent together and time you can't get back.

more than anything love is attention to the small
things and how they make us feel.

like how i always fall asleep during road trips no
matter how long they are.

and how i will sacrifice anything to spend more time
with the people that i love.

love is attention,
love is attention to the things that really matter.

A Personal Poem

Trinity Rivers

Harmony of Expressions

In Flint's heart, Southwest Classical Academy,
Where trials brewed like storms in troubled sea.
'Midst mace and struggles, I fought to rise,
Yet found no beacon 'neath desolate skies.

A guiding hand emerged, amidst the shifting sands,
Leading me forth to where my destiny stands.
Now, at U of M Flint, I take my grand leap,
With newfound strength, my own path to keep.

With Black Student Union, I've carved foreseen shifting sand,
Through empowering voices and shattering boundaries, I go.

Empowering voices as a champion for mental health,
In collegiate realms, I strive for more and more,
breaking barriers whilst dared to soar,

A Personal Essay

Satya Randolph

Harmony of Expressions

My academic journey has been the most roller coaster experience I have ever gone through. School has not only shaped my desired outcome in life, but it has shaped me personally, something I never thought would happen. During my early childhood experiences with school, I was known as the "talkative one". My teachers would always write on my report card, "smart, but TALKATIVE" and yes, talkative in all caps as though they were trying to emphasize that it is an ongoing problem.

I have always had a passion for learning and growing in every which way, but it soon spiraled down once I reached 5th grade leading into middle school. Although I was talkative, I was also showing laziness in my work at a very young age and it soon grew with me. It stuck with me throughout my whole academic journey and caused a lot of mishaps in my education. Although I had a passion for learning, I began to experience the "easy way out" of everything and I even began it personally as well. Late work, not turning in work, not studying, not taking my academic journey seriously began to take a toll on me. My parents were always on me and my brothers regarding our grades and when I soon figured the bad grades weren't getting me anywhere I started settling for the "passing grades".

Throughout my middle school years, all I really cared about was playing the violin and dance, and I had a deep passion for both. My parents would tell me that if my grades weren't up, I wouldn't be able to participate in either and that brung me to want to get "passing grades". I carried that throughout highschool and soon landed myself on the 'academic probation list". It scared me badly because not only would I fail my dream school, Genesee Early College, but my parents would find out and be extremely disappointed in me. And I didn't want that to happen.

So, I began going to tutoring, because it was required, and began trying to bring my grades up, but I was so far behind that it didn't matter what I did, I still would have ended up failing. At that point, I was lost, and made up in my mind that I just had to accept the fate that was handed to me. I couldn't believe myself. For all the hard work that my parents embedded in me only for me to not take it seriously and fail out of school. At that point, it was crucial for me to get enrolled in another school as soon as possible. That's when we came across Mott Middle High School. It was the same type of curriculum, except I got to choose the degree I wanted to major in, which was exciting to me. As I began the program, I noticed myself falling back into the same habits, but this time I actually began to create a deep passion into my future career.

My careers shifted so much, from wanting to be a lawyer, to a detective, to even switching genres and going into the healthcare field and becoming a doctor. It was so much I wanted to do with my life, until I fully sat down and learned more about myself on a personal level and figured out what my likes and dislikes were. I began to meet some new people in high school that would either serve as a lesson in my

Harmony of Expressions

life or a blessing, either way I had two options; either reciprocate what I promised myself I wouldn't do anymore or push myself and focus on the bigger picture, and from then on I went to change my major and soon graduate with my General Studies degree and also maintaining a 3.4 GPA while also completing half my bachelor's degree, which I am currently finishing up and soon to graduate with my BSN.

Throughout my journey, I began to tie my personal and academic life together, because without strength in one, there was not going to be any growth in the other. And from then on I began taking my studies seriously and learning that I am the one in charge of my fate and my success, and if I really want it, I have to prove it and work even harder to get it.

A Poem
Anonymous

Harmony of Expressions

Deciding to earn a great tomorrow
You give up your today
Take part in a four year journey
And find friends along the way
Give an hour to them
Get a day of freedom
Ignoring a due date
Leaves the stress seldom
After a month of repeating
Something starts to overflow
Inside you really know
You gave up your tomorrow

A Personal Essay
Josiah Trzil

Harmony of Expressions

When covid began I was not super bothered by all of the changes. At the time, the idea of not having to go to school and being stuck at home didn't sound so bad. I remember playing video games with my friend everyday. I remember being on long, enjoyable phone calls with my friends throughout this time and I began to adapt to this new way of communication. I also found ways to keep things interesting so I wasn't just sitting in my pajamas all day. I would get dressed everyday, even though I was staying at home, just so I add some flavor to my day. Soon the school system started implementing a hybrid form of education. Since they couldn't keep everyone in school for five days a week, they would take half of the school on Monday's and Friday's and the other half would come on Tuesdays' and Thursday's. With Wednesday being in the middle of the week it felt really nice to sleep in and not have a whole lot of school work to do. Some teachers would schedule extra zoom calls on Wednesday's, just to go over the material more, which was beneficial for classes like Accounting or Business Administration. Speaking of Zoom, I became very familiar with this platform throughout 2020. Every teacher used this platform as a means of communication, and it worked quite effectively. Once the school year finished, I really didn't have a whole lot to do. I remember being bored of playing video games, and watching tv was getting boring and I needed to shake things up. I needed a new hobby, I had played soccer all of my life, but I was getting to the point where I wanted to focus more on my close friendships and my fitness. I had also had bad past experiences with soccer teams, so I just started running on my own or with my friend. This was fun for awhile but I really just wanted to belong to a community of people. I was graduating in May of 2021 and I knew that I wasn't going to be close with most people from school because I wasn't going to see them as much anymore. And I had also been going to church on Sunday's & Wednesday's my entire life, but I was never really a big fan. However, one time on a Wednesday I decided to try it out and participate in the event they put on. And it ended up changing everything for me. After that night, I got as involved as I could and joined their internship. It was then that I learned many key lessons that I still apply to my everyday life.

Things like Servanthood Leadership, showing Honor to those who have earned it, being Respectful and Sensitive, etc. The church not only provided me with a community of loving and accepting people, They also helped me refine myself into a leader. I wouldn't be who I am today without the church. And even though covid was terrible and the cause of many unfortunate deaths, it helped me get my life on track, and for that I am thankful.

Education In Spite of Segregation

Andre D. Powell II

Harmony of Expressions

Let me tell you about HBCUs, 107 children that were outcasts of our institutional society. All `have a unique name and an ordained and divine purpose. Triumph is their middle name, a sacred and glorious term that eloquently symbolizes their future.

Historically, black colleges and universities aka HBCU. HBCUs have been doing more for the African American community. For you see it has produced More black doctors, pharmacists, lawyers, and black teachers. In fact, HBCU produces 51.6 % of African-Americans that obtained agriculture degrees. So are they really outcasts? It is a known fact that Black students who had at least one black teacher in elementary school, are more likely to succeed in their education. HBCU students helped define the term success by overcoming social and economic obstacles in spite of segregation. In the current day there's still work to be done as we climb towards equality.

Although faced with adversity. On February 25th,1837, Cheyney University of Pennsylvania emerged through the fire by becoming the first Historically Black College and University paving the way for many more after. A beam of hope and a light of change. A victory for one and a challenge for others. Did you know that the 62nd United States colored infantry founded Lincoln University of Missouri? This same group helped African Americans in the state of Missouri learn vital skills for combat to help aid the US during the civil war. Ohio got its Historically black land grant institution, Central

State University in 1887. 1890 Historically Black Land-Grant Universities were some of the first Historically Black Colleges and Universities (HBCUs) in the country, according to the Second Morrill Act, which obliged former Confederate states to build sister universities for Blacks. Central State University is one of the notable 19 land grant institutions.

History informs us that The Christan Church Disciples of Christ didn't want to be left out of this great change and founded Jarvis Christian College in 1912. Institutions like Jarvis Christian College were important in the civil rights era because they were used as gathering locations for the African American community. The modern term would be what we call a safe space. On the campus of Shaw University on April 15, 1960, Dr. Martin Luther King Jr. spoke to an assembly of roughly 200 students.
" Located in the land of golden sunshine there is Tennessee State University. My favorite hbcu. Who is 109 years old. Tennessee State University embodies its motto: "Think, Work, and Serve." Found on the great Holliday of Juneteenth (June 19) in the year 1912. The holiday is used to pay homage to the last group of slaves to be freed witch were in the lone star state of Texas During the battle of segregation, the roaring sound of feet marching on the streets of Greensboro was just the start for four North Carolina Agricultural and Technical State University students who sat down at a counter in a white-only restaurant, sparking a movement of equality that would go down in history.

Harmony of Expressions

This movement is now known as the Greensboro sit-in. Which brought together many hbcu students from all across the county to help fight for change. The students helped inspire other HBCUs students to do the same in their own communities. Present-day the HBCUs are still fighting for respect amongst Predominantly White Institutions aka PWI. In 1965 HBCUs were finally recognized as premier institutions of higher education making them equal to PWIs. Thanks to the Higher Education Act of 1965. Even with the Higher Education Act of 1965, HBCUs are still not treated as equals. You can see examples of injustice and inequality in media stories over time about the government's misappropriation of funds and resources for HBCUs. when things are supposed to be presented as both education systems. Making equality inclusiveness and diversity for all people. This is the most accurate depiction of an HBCU.

Works Cited

Alumni. "History." Tennessee State University, www.tnstate.edu/library/digitalresources/centennial/history/.

"HBCU Facts." Cleveland Council of Black Colleges Alumni Association, www.hbcualumnicle.com/hbcu-facts.html.

"History & Traditions." Cheyney University of Pennsylvania, 17 Jan. 2020, cheyney.edu/for-parents/history-traditions/.

"Home." Central State University, www.centralstate.edu/academics/cse/agriculture/index.php?. "JCC Facts." Jarvis Christian College | Hawkins TX, East Texas, www.jarvis.edu/jcc-facts. "Our History." Lincoln University of Missouri - Lincoln University, www.lincolnu.edu/web/about-lincoln/our-history.

My 2023-2024 Journey
Zachary Palmer

Harmony of Expressions

Firstly, I want it to be known that before I start to talk about everything lets go ahead and put a disclaimer out there for the people who will actually read this, I AM NO LONGER THE WAY THAT I'M TALKING ABOUT HERE. Now that that is out of the way, enjoy my chaotic 9 months. And another thing, the 9 months does NOT indicate what you think it indicates. Ziggy is too busy, broke, and pretty to have a child. Not in this economy. Anyway, enjoy the trainwreck.

Where do I start? How about here, July 2023 is the month when I lost the love of my life. I know what you're thinking, you're thinking that statement couldn't possibly be the truth, but I assure you it was. With a tear in my eye and anxiety in my heart, I watched as she walked out of that proverbial door. Leaving me with my heart in my pocket, along with my wallet and her engagement ring that I was waiting for the right moment to strike with. I got through the best that I could, but I had a her-sized hole in my heart that just couldn't be filled (even today). But I was still there for her whenever she needed me. Until…

September comes around, I make sure that her first semester in college is a good one as if I was still with her. But I could never imagine that she would hug me and tell me that she still wanted to be with me. After a short vacation, she came back completely changed. She only loved me as a friend when she got back but I would come whenever she asked for me still. But all of that ended on Christmas Eve. She had told me that she had been with someone else. Started talking to him a week after she left me. That entire time, I was fighting for second place in a race that didn't even exist.

January, it's her birthday. She invites me out and we're having the time of our lives. It starts to feel like the old days when we BOTH loved each other. Everything seemed like it was back to the way it was, she even almost kissed me again. You'd think that's where all this madness would end right? Well, sir or madame, this story isn't how I got my almost wife back. She tells me that she had a good time, hugs me, and goes home. We had a falling-out over text that night. Coupled with other major problems in my house at the time, it made me spiral with feelings that I hadn't felt in years. (Here's where that disclaimer was needed), January 4th, 2024, 2:34 AM, I attempted to leave this planet.

Skipping forward, It's the months afterward, I was struggling, and I was getting tired of telling people (falsely) that I was okay. I haven't been okay for a very long time now. This pain is much too real. Luckily, I had great friends. The point that I'm making with this essay is that life is going to simply beat the brakes off of you and people will expect you to smile through it. You just have to get used to being kicked and told you're worthless until you triumph. I'm nowhere near the triumph stage but I'll tell you one thing, you forget a thousand things every day, how about you make sure this is one of them. Goodbye and goodnight.

My COVID-19 Lockdown Days

Davis Ouedraogo

Harmony of Expressions

My Lockdown days during the COVID-19 pandemic were not really that much exciting to be honest. In fact, most days felt kinda boring. On one hand, I got to spend more time with my family. On the other hand, there was nothing exciting to do but just stay cooped up inside my house all day. And as each day passed, it felt like time was moving slower and slower. The Lockdown lasted for so long that I thought the pandemic was never going to end at first. And all I could think about throughout the lockdown was how this all started.

I remember it like it was yesterday, for me it all started on the day of Thursday, March 12th, 2020. All that time I was only a sophomore in high school, and that Thursday was our last day of school right before everything got shut down. That next day on Friday morning, my parents got a call from school saying that the school was gonna be closed for the next few days. At first I didn't know why the school was closed for a few days, until later that day when I watched the news. The news reported that schools across the nation were shutting down and going to be quarantined for a few days due to rapidly growing cases of people getting sick from an unknown illness that was later known as the coronavirus or COVID-19 for short.

During those few days quarantined at home from school, I decided to take that time as an opportunity for me to just kick back and relax. At first I thought that, because I thought it was just going to be a few days at home and that things would be back to normal in no time. But just when I thought things were going to get better, it got really worse very fast. On the last night of the supposite few day quarantine, I felt relaxed and ready to go back to school. But just as I was about to prepare for school the next day, I got an email from school that night saying that the school was going to be closed and that we were going to be quarantined for another week by order of the state due to growing COVID-19 cases.

After that, it seemed like everything was getting worse by the day. Because so many people were catching the coronavirus, the state just kept extending the quarantine. First a week turned into 2 weeks, then 2 weeks became one month, and finally one month turned into a 3 month total statewide quarantine lockdown. Because of the 3 month lockdown, almost everything was shut down such as schools, most restaurants, and most grocery stores. I just couldn't believe that this was actually happening.

Even though we had to stay indoors throughout the lockdown, I just tried to do everything I could to maintain my mental health. So for the first month of quarantine, I did a lot of the things I would normally do on a typical weekend. I spent time with my family, watched some movies, played video games, and even read some books. And every once in a while I would just step outside my front door for a few minutes just to catch some sun and fresh air. Towards the end of the first month of quarantine, I got an email from my school saying that we would be switching to virtual learning to finish out the school year.

Harmony of Expressions

For the last two months of quarantine which was also the last two months of the school year, I had to spend some time on my computer Monday thru Friday working on schoolwork from home and doing weekly zoom sessions with my teachers. At first I was a little bit skeptical about doing school from home, because I didn't know what this would mean for my mental health. But when I first started school from home, I realized that working from home was great starting out, because I was able to do things that I couldn't normally do on a school day such as sleeping in a little later, being able to stay in my pajamas or comfy clothes, and not having to start school until 8am each morning. And on top of everything else, I was able to finish all of my work on time, get good grades, and still have the rest of the day to relax.

In conclusion, I've learned that there were some good and bad things about the pandemic and lockdown. The good thing was that I got to have some more free time and spend some time with family. On the other hand, the bad thing was the fact that I had to stay indoors 24 hours a day and 7 days a week for 3 months . But overall, this pandemic and lockdown has taught me about the importance of maintaining my mental health and being able to see the positive side of things. And that no matter how bad a situation may seem, you must try to keep pushing forward.

A Personal Essay

Eyona Numan

Harmony of Expressions

My name is Eyona Numan and I am currently in my senior year at University of Michigan-Flint. I am 20 years old and will turn 21 in May of 2024. One event that I would like to share in my life would be when I first entered foster care at the age of 12. While the story I am about to tell is inspiring, I am going to put a trigger warning because I am going to discuss a heavy topic.

First, let's start with the present day and what I am doing currently that is benefiting me on my journey to recovering from depression. I am a person who is recovering from depression and sticking to my treatment goals of being healthier and happier. While things do get hard every once in a while, my ultimate goal is to be a happy and successful adult in the community. For me, the one thing that has helped me since day one is my faith in Jesus Christ.

While things are better now, I have been in a dark place before as a child. There was a time where I was self-harming as a child and that was a big move to make for someone my age. One thing I can tell you about my childhood is that I was emotionally abused and I couldn't get help for it at the time. Until, one day, something had changed and I attempted suicide at the age of 12. However, someone had noticed that I was going through a rough time because I was in the hospital not really trying to say what was wrong. When I got to the actual place where they had put an IV in me, this was around the time that I had told the nurse what was really going on.

Additionally, everything from there on got better once I was admitted into a psychiatric hospital, away

from the abuse and was finally able to breathe. However, that doesn't mean that I wasn't apprehensive at first when they had administered anti-psychotic medicine and was trying not to take it. Then, I had eventually talked to my doctor and he made me less apprehensive and as a kid, that was very rewarding for someone to treat me as an adult of sound and mind. I
eventually got permanently removed from my parents and this was when I had entered foster care. Fast forward to the present day, I remember every single detail about that life-changing event and how I managed to find help in the most mysterious way possible. I wasn't expecting a nurse to help me because I had tried to contact CPS and tell a therapist but it was to no avail. To this day, I wonder what my life would have been like if that nurse didn't notice what I was going through. For me, it was also a test of faith and putting all of my trust into the Lord. Now, I am about to age out of foster care on my 21st birthday and while this is about to be the end of this chapter, this is also going to be the beginning of a new chapter in my life and I am pretty excited about what I see already.

A Personal Essay
J'Kobe Moore

Harmony of Expressions

Growing up I had plenty of trials and tribulations that I went through. I grew up in a single-parent household with my mother and two siblings. I felt like I had to grow up fast because I felt the need to become the "man" of the house. Growing up I was taught about many stereotypes that men have to do such as don't cry, don't share what you go through and how you feel, don't express yourself, and many other typical stereotypes. I started to drift away from that boy who was always happy, and friendly. I became angrier, I began to not care about school and people who I should be caring for, I also did things I had no business doing. I was doing things such as hanging with certain people and fighting all the time. But the turning point I had with this was when my grandfather told me that he was disappointed in me, that he didn't understand me, that he worried about me, and that he just didn't know about me. When he said he didn't know about me it meant that he didn't know what I was gone do in life and where I was heading if I didn't clean up my act. These words struck me and stood with me for a while and to be honest they still do to this day because he is somebody that I look up to. Imagine somebody who you look at as a role model/ hero and they tell you that they are disappointed in you… it's not a pleasant feeling. It was then that I decided it was time to change. I was tired of hearing about how people were so disappointed in me, and I was tired of having people worry about me. I began to become more spiritual and read my bible more than ever. I felt that if I wanted to change mentally and physically it would have to start spiritually. The bible verse Job 37:12-13 "They turn around and around by his guidance, to accomplish all that he commands them on the face of the habitable world. Whether for correction or for his land or for love, he causes it to happen." And Philippians 4:13 "I can do all things through Christ who strengthens me." These Bible verses helped guide me into the way I wanted to go. These Bible verses helped guide me into the way I wanted to go. I started to notice that the things that were once holding me hostage were starting to fade away. I started to feel like I was becoming myself again. My attitude toward school and life shifted. It was all thanks to my Grandad, my mentors, and most importantly God. I am thankful for having people in my corner who stuck by me when times were tough. They all believed in me when I didn't believe in myself. Now I am an honor student with 2 degrees working on my third one. I always heard how just one conversation with someone can change your life, but I didn't believe it until I went through it.

Untitled

Isabella Modrak

Harmony of Expressions

P atience and
R esillience are the
O nly tools we need for **S** uccess, but don't forget
that **P** erquisites can be just as **E** jectable without the
R espect cultivated by
I ntegrity developed
T hrough paving
Y our own path.

- Isabella Modrak

A Poem

Jamiah McQuiller

Harmony of Expressions

To know yourself is to hear the call
To choose yourself is to answer
March 2019 they said to stay inside,
To face my past, my life,
There was no where else to hide
I looked in the mirror only to find a pre- painted portrait of me every time.
A predetermined height, never to grow?
A portrait embodying my pre determined worth, but how could anyone know? Pre packaged thoughts, like "black women are so strong"
Made it difficult for me to be comfortable asking for help later on
When I looked at other portraits, to learn and explore, and see There was always a blatant and deliberate lack in diversity
Every picture of red roses were white washed, Imagine that,
then painted every other color of the rainbow ,except for brown and black "Too loud" "too lazy" "affirmative action"
And a bunch of other micro aggressive attacks
Is this who I am? Or all I'll ever be?
I felt more in my heart, and mind, and soul
My thoughts raced at light speed
But what if? And how could? And maybe if I try
Then the pre painted portrait began to fade
What I saw before me was alive
It moved like me, and showed the truth
Of my essence, beauty and the world behind my eyes
With that, self love began to rise, pour into my soul, a ball

McQuiller

And then again, my inner phone rang, and I heard the call
A baby, they said, 9 months then there was a baby girl
When I held her first, every doubt and fear, vanished from my world
She looked at me as a protector, in the would she would explore, and rise in after every fall
And in that moment, just like before I began to hear the call
I could not let her mirror be muddled with pre painted limitations I pour love and limitless beliefs into her so she won't fall prey to imitations
Seeds planted in my soul began to sprout, I was excited for them to bloom
But I was not expecting to entertain the thoughts that my mind would be full of soon
I began taking online classes, in cyber security, tech
Single mother, black woman, from a low income background But there was hope yet
Despite the intentionally crippling truths of my academic childhood that were all around:
Lack of access to quality resources, insufficient funding for my local schools But that didn't hold me down
In a predominantly white male dominated industry, with no representation, implicit biases , and unequal pathways for career growth, but an industry in its prime
And a child at home, who is ready to eat
Is it worth the time?
It was tiring, to say the least

Harmony of Expressions

Pandemic, Online classes, bills and more bills
Hiring seemed obsolete
I was under qualified, over qualified, or the tech company was a scam I poured half of me into my child, and tech got the other half of all that I am I kept going, I kept learning, I kept yearning for more
I wasn't trying to break through ceilings yet,
But I was busting open doors
My mind's eye, a playground, possibilities never ending
And then I learned, from my daughter of course, the power in pretending
Then again began the "what if"s and "how about"
Now I drive my daughter to school, in my car
Then send her off with love, from a mother's heart
Then I drive myself to the University of Michigan-Flint to be everything I've ever dreamed
Generational curse breaker, way maker, black girl magic, representation on the tech scene
I am collaborating to bring 4D medical models and scans into Virtual environments
So that surgeons and doctors can better analyze data that's ground breaking
To the child in me, to my child, to the one's who look like me, There are no limits but the once you accept
Your place in the world is yours for the taking
Consider me represented
To know yourself is to hear the call
To choose yourself is to answer

UM-Flint Changed My Life

Anthony Malone

Harmony of Expressions

When you think of college you may think that it's just there to further your education. And while it did further my education, and progress my knowledge of vast topics it also saved and changed my life. It's allowed me to further my growth as a person, leader, and even worker. This has a few reasons, the most important: the KCP Program, Interaction outside of the classroom, Student Life, and so much more.

King Chavez Parks… Where do I even start, when I came to college 2 years ago it was crazy to think the program was titled Promise Scholars. It was a program to take a chance on low-GPA individuals like myself in high school and give them the chance to succeed and strive in college. By giving us the resources, and a bridge from high school to college. In the form of workshops and classes in the summer time, this bridge got us across to college and ready for a lot of the challenges first-year students face on a day-to-day basis.

Struggles such as procrastination, navigating the campus, finding resources and so much more. This program is what gave all of us the resources to transition to college.

Following this another thing that changed me was the interaction with professors out of the classroom. There's plenty of interaction on the university campus. Faculty are very easy to find and make time with, as the class sizes are no larger than 30-40 at the biggest level on our campus. This means that our interactions with professors are more unique, and more personalized to us rather than being a tick on a piece of paper with 300 students.

This interaction breeds great student-professor relationships that I can say I've benefited from as being able to get in contact with my professors at a moment's notice makes my life very easy, and less stressful come finals week.

Finally, the thing I love most about our campus is our campus life. For a campus this small you would think that our campus life is irrelevant, and sure on some days it's not that busy but I can confidently say that Monday - Thursday our campus is alive and well. There are always events going on by numerous student organizations and even some faculty-run organizations/resources. The University Center (UCEN) being the main hub of it all houses a lot of the resources on campus and houses some event rooms/centers where events are held. Without this building our campus wouldn't be as lively. I owe a lot of my best memories to the UCEN as that's a place I spend a lot of my time religiously.

In conclusion The University of Michigan - Flint has changed my life. By providing me with so many different resources, and giving me a guide of where I want to go in life. Giving me the guarantee that no matter what there's always someone I can talk to about anything, and also allowing me to find people to connect with, through various student organizations and clubs. I owe so much to this university. GO BLUE!

Navigating Loss & Finding Strength Amidst The Epidemic

Angel Maldonado

Harmony of Expressions

As a Mexican-American navigating the intricacies of culture, identity, and community, my journey has been influenced by a tapestry of triumphs and challenges. However, none have had the same deep or transforming impact as the COVID-19 epidemic, which not only challenged my resilience but also transformed the fundamental fabric of my existence. In the middle of this global disaster, I found myself facing personal challenges exacerbated by the loss of my loving grandparents, whose deaths during the epidemic threw a pull over our family. Despite the depths of grief, the value of cultural heritage, and the enduring strength of familial relationships. In discussing my experiences with overcoming difficulties during the COVID-19 epidemic, I wish to highlight the common themes of loss, love, and perseverance that bind us all in our humanity.

Growing up in a close-knit Mexican American household, my grandparents were important in molding my identity and beliefs. They were the foundation of our family, representing knowledge, tenderness, and endless love. However, the COVID-19 epidemic presented unexpected obstacles that tested our familial relationships and strength. The epidemic not only endangered physical health but also caused emotional and psychological harm, particularly for those who had lost loved ones. My grandparents, while not directly affected by COVID-19, fell victim to its collateral effects. The epidemic's seclusion and disturbance worsened their pre-existing health issues, resulting in their deaths.

Their departure created a tremendous vacuum in our family, sending us into a sea of pain and uncertainty.

While navigating the tumultuous waves of loss, I found consolation in the strength of our familial bonds and the resilience ingrained in our cultural history. We honored the memory of loved ones through bright celebrations of life, drawing from the rich tapestry of Mexican American customs. The notion of "Dia de los Muertos" serves as a poignant reminder of the ongoing tie between the living and the gone. Amidst the depths of sadness, I discovered a renewed respect for life's brief moments and the value of cherishing the time we have with people we care about. The epidemic served as a sobering reminder of the fragility of life and the need of living each day with appreciation and meaning.In the face of hardship, I went on a path of self-discovery and personal development, turning my grief into good action. Through acts of compassion and community service, I hoped to respect my grandparents' legacy and support those who were most vulnerable during the pandemic's turmoil. Whether I was helping at a local food bank or just listening to people in need, service and solidarity brought me healing.

As the globe begins to emerge from the shadow of the epidemic, I take with me the lessons learned and the resilience built in the crucible of hardship. Though the scars of loss may persist, they serve as a monument to the depth of love and the human spirit's ability to endure the darkest of circumstances. Adversity may weave threads of sadness and

Harmony of Expressions

anguish into the fabric of life, but it is through the collective power of community, the tenacity of the human spirit, and the eternal links of love that we find the bravery to rise above and construct a better tomorrow.

Finding My Way To the Light

Jalon Kirks

Harmony of Expressions

Kirks

Every year I would have this heart-racing suspense watching the big colored crystal LED New Year ball drop from New York City live at Times Square on TV with my mom. Just as the crowd on the TV counted down "5, 4, 3, 2, 1," my heart began to race big for this year. And the clock strikes 12:00 midnight, January 1, 2017 – Happy New Year! The year of my dream is finally here. I realized when those numbers lit up on the TV screen that this would be the year to start preparing for the real world because this is the year that I am going to be graduating high school and going off to college! I just knew this would be the year everything would pay off and be filled with much happiness and joy, but I also didn't know what else the year would bring and where things would go and turn out after encountering some unexpected news….25 days just after the new year, my mom broke the news that her father, my grandfather passed away, my first grandparent gone.

My mother is a strong woman and it saddened me to see her upset and heartbroken because this was a devastating experience for both of us. From then I would make sure I hang in there with her and help her to the end, so moving forward I continued to finish strong during high school and just before I am close to graduating, the mayflowers began to bloom. I was a first time prom king my senior year in high school and graduating in the top 5 of my class year were the greatest accomplishments to experience and leave a mark from! After a restful summer, here I am now approaching my first experience at the University of Michigan-Flint as a first generation freshman student in the fall of 2017. This is finally it…I have graduated high school and now realized that it was time to adapt to a new city, a new life, new diversity and new experience.

I was pretty bashful and overwhelmed with adjusting to a new urban lifestyle and getting to know everyone and my roommates but as the time rolled I began to open up and start navigating myself around new people and areas of Flint. I even got used to shopping on my own and learned to commute on my own with public transportation like the University shuttle and the Greyhound to home to visit my family on breaks. 2017 was definitely an eye-opening year for me and despite of the rain, I knew that God was in control, speaking of, I began to know more about Jesus as I joined the University of Michigan Flint's Intervarsity Christian Fellowship in September 2017 and also attended their first Compelling Event in November 2017 and I found the whole experience amazing because I haven't been to church in a while, so I wanted to take the opportunity to reconnect with Jesus throughout my college experience.

For my first semester as a freshman, I was prepared on how difficult the courses would be but as I learned to manage my time and assignments of my classes, I actually enjoyed them all, the biggest challenge of one of my course was Intro to Public Speaking as a freshman because I don't really talk as much and I did not know much about Public Speaking. Another class that I enjoyed the most was

Taboo Language because I got to learn the history of swearing words in society. I thought that those two courses played a role into my beginning of adulthood because in the real world communication and terminology is important.

My winter semester vs my fall semester was more difficult and challenging, although I just had got the hang of adapting to Flint. As the semester was approaching to the end I figured, I need to enjoy myself more before we all start to pack and leave campus for the summer. I started going to more social events around campus and enjoyed the last memories of the semester in my dorm at First Street with my roommates and other dorm peers.

As the semester finally came to an end I decided to continue with a summer course at a community college at my hometown Muskegon. Muskegon Community College has been a junior college for Muskegon students who choose to attend junior college to obtain an associates degree before transferring to an official university or college. For me it was a tough decision between Muskegon Community College and University of Michigan-Flint, however I convinced myself that a better experience would be at a better University which I chose to attend the University of Michigan-Flint and I am glad that I chose to have a better experience with my college journey because I do not regret every moment worth making memories.

But as for the summer I've continued my education to take a math course in placement of a math course at University of Michigan-Flint to transfer

Harmony of Expressions

my transcript to my home university. This was another challenging experience because not only did I need to focus on passing my course to stay on track but I also needed to secure my finances so I went about searching for summer employment but there was no luck on finding any openings in enough time to have the funds to cover my semester next year. However, I managed to remain focused on nailing my summer math course and it was successful and I passed my course with the grade that I needed to transfer back to UM-Flint.

As I began to humbly prepare myself for my sophomore year at U of M, I ran into an adversity in terms of funds…This year indeed was not going to be the same as my freshman year and I realized that this was the time to buckle down and take my next remain class years more seriously. My tuition for my sophomore year was more steep than my freshman year but I was offered an option to apply for a University loan known as the parent plus loan. I told myself that at some point I am going to need a job to cover my expenses for the next few years plus nail my classes. So here I am in my sophomore year and discovered that it was time to roll up my sleeves and prepare to work hard with my classes.

I also started getting to know my areas more in Flint and around the campus, I was now living in my second University residence - Riverfront around Saginaw St. but knew things were different compared to my freshman year. I was taking my first math class at UM-Flint and as the semester continued, my sophomore year was beginning to become filled with challenging tasks in terms of my math course and quite stressful. So to do damage control I needed to get the help from my tutor to pass the courses because failing was not an option.

I know it has been a minute since I've known the concepts of math since my high school years but it just took time to refresh my memory to utilize the methods to apply for the college intermediate algebra course skills. My other courses were not so bad, but through it all I also wanted to enjoy my second year of college. I got the hang of actually navigating my way around the University, visiting my family and became more independent as part of being a responsible adult.

So continuing on from my Fall break down to the middle of the semester, I received an unexpected news from my mother that my grandmother suffered from her first stroke. My grandmother was a wise woman who me, my mom and my family knew all our lives. She was filled with humor, love and joy and she was strong willed. I enjoyed all the memories from a baby to an adult with her, so it bothered me from that shocking news and I actually made audio memories of her during the summer of 2018, and I actually did not regret making these memories as I should because tomorrow is never promised to anyone. Sometimes I wish I could turn back the hands of time and make more memories, because to hear that news began to give me acute depression. However I definitely needed to check on her and so I gave her a call as I normally would from time to time to check on her and my mother. Thankfully she

Harmony of Expressions

recovered in less than 24 hours, I was also thankful and grateful that she was still alive!

I continued on with the semester and prepared for a new year and a new semester, although it was not easy but I managed to try my best and not give up. Here we are down to a new year - January 1, 2019, the last year of the 2010s decade. I just knew this would be the year of peace, joy and happiness, but to my perspective it was giving hints of 2017 again. Me and my mom abruptly discovered that my grandmother suffered her second stroke 5 days later from the new year…This time, I had to pray to give her another chance because we cannot lose her – my second grandparent from my mother's side… Thankfully the heavenly father, gave her another chance and she recovered once again! This time I was more thankful as well as my family.

It was time to rock and roll to the fullest and knock the next semester out of the park. Overall, my sophomore year was a challenge in terms of my courses. I won't exactly say I was facing what they call the "Sophomore Slump" but I just knew it was time to do better with my grades. I was home for the summer for a second time and decided that I'm going to keep the ball rolling and stay on top of it. Just as I was hoping this summer would be the best, I was in for another devastating news that rocked me, my mom and my family to the core…May 7, 2019, me and my mother did not hear from my grandmother as we normally would. My mother would call her everyday after coming home from work. After not hearing from her we went to her apartment together in time to rush her to the hospital after suffering her final stroke. My family and I prayed and prayed that she can recover once again from this horrible accident…Unfortunately she did not recover from her final stroke and sadly passed away on May 10, 2019. We loved my grandmother, I knew her all my life and experiencing her tragic accident to her death was a huge blow for me and the family. This was going to be a death that affected me mentally and emotionally for a very long time or forever, especially for my mother…This was the first depressing and emotional summer to experience because it was no longer going to be the same as the previous summers.

However I managed to find the strength to find summer employment at a global automotive company - Shape Corporation. This was a big step for me because this was going to be my first official work experience that I can include in my resume and get some real world work experience. I was finally able to work throughout the summer to have the finances to secure my tuition for my continuing sophomore year. Returning back to UM-Flint for the fall of 2019 was going to be different for me in terms of my mental health and grieving time. It was also going to give me breathing room because me and my other roommates were going to have our own single bedrooms which was interesting and I enjoyed having my own space. It was the perfect time to have in my room to process my emotions and grief from my grandmother and just take time to have for myself before mingling around campus. Although it was

Harmony of Expressions

mentally rough, I managed to pick up the slack on my course grades and also look for scholarships for next semester and the following year. I managed to pass all of my courses for Fall 2019 and was ready to come back harder than I left.

A new year and a new decade has arrived – January 1, 2020. Just as we are all now in a new decade, surely no one knew what 2020 would bring until a few months later. For me it had already begun a rough year because I was in a hole of debt for my Winter 2020 tuition. My courses and my start if the semester was already becoming stressful, however I managed to dig up funds from my first on-campus job working as a Housing & Front Desk Assistant to pay for my semester also with the help from my mother. I then realized that it was necessary to always have employment and enough funds to cover debt even in the beginning of my 20s because it is a part of being responsible in the real world. Months later no one in the world could catch a break as we all encountered our first pandemic of the COVID-19 outbreak in March 2020.

When I thought that 2019 would be such a scary year in the new year and down, the most frustrating, horrible time of our lives would come in 2020, that we would consider the worst year ever… Things had shifted upside down, everyone began to panic and shopped in every store to stock up on housing necessities to be safe from this horrible outbreak affecting everyone's lives and health. All universities had transitioned to virtual-learning and it became very frustrating and stressful for all of us college students. There was no telling how long we were going to deal with this terrible moment of our lives. It was very hard to focus through online learning because I had to get used to virtual learning for the first time away from the university. Through stress, anxiety, and depression (S.A.D.), I needed to find some occupational activities to do during this pandemic. I am a pretty good cook so I would prepare good meals to cook and eat during the time, really good meals.

After my grandmother passed away I decided that this would be a perfect time to start a diary or everyday journal, even good memories from the past. Speaking of, I began a memory hobby creating a "memory box" with certain seasonal memories of the year. I would create multiple folders of a season of year like "Fall 2017", "Fall 2018", "Fall 2019" and then add videos from my fall years in their own folder to revisit the fun memories of the past when times were hard during the pandemic. I even created childhood memory albums to go back in time to reminisce the fun memories during my childhood. I even dwelled in good memories from the 2010s wishing I could go back like the rest. Some people wished they could go back to 2019…I wished I could go back to 2009 so that we could relive 2010s all over again because 2019 was too close to 2020 involving my grandmother's death…No way!

My mother told me that when I was a baby that she would take me anywhere that I would like to go or anywhere in the world. So in August 2020, I was asked if I wanted to take a trip to New Orleans and have my first plane ride. I agreed and after I took my first trip with my mother to New Orleans, I did not regret the opportunity. This was also my first time in New Orleans so there was a lot to explore and learn from and more, but it was also an opportunity that I would not change.

After enjoying the memories looking back at New Orleans, we decided to take another trip to Las Vegas around my mother's birthday and it was a lovely experience for the first time and I thought that we should go again. I felt like it was a great opportunity for both of us to get away from the past trauma of my grandmother's death and it was a nice way to end 2020. When the new year came to end in 2020 – January 1, 2021, we just knew everything would get better in time and we prayed at the strike of midnight and thanked the Lord. This new year that everyone thought would be better than 2020 could not get any worse.

2021 had begun to be a living nightmare for all of us, especially for me because just as we were going to take another trip to Las Vegas after mother's day, my mother caught COVID-19 in May. I had to do everything in my power to take care of her, because all I could think of was "I CANNOT lose my mother" behind my grandmother, and my grandfather! I was trying to maintain my online courses and my summer course I took after Spring 2021 for Muskegon Community College. This was an uphill battle to conquer my courses and remain positive mentally and emotionally. I prayed that my mother would recover and weeks later by the grace of God she recovered from COVID 19 and we were blessed with continuing to survive and enjoy life! I was so thankful she is still alive because the COVID-19 virus & pandemic has been far worse than death for all of us.

We continued to take more trips and make more memories while caring for our health. Tomorrow is NEVER promised for anyone! This was the big takeaway during this pandemic experience. After 2022 arrived I began to start preparing to return to campus after battling my online courses. Me and my mother were already vaccinated to be protected from this horrible virus no one wants to experience. During the summer of 2022 I began to go back to employment after receiving two years of unemployment benefits. I worked with my mother at her job for the first time at Shape Corporation at a different plant to rebuild my finances for my tuition when I returned to campus after two years of quarantine.

I have finally returned back to the campus of University of Michigan-Flint for the Fall of 2022, I have updated my major from being a Mechanical Engineering to Digital Manufacturing Technology and also became part of the College of Technology Innovation as an CIT student, so here is a new year, new major and new beginning for me. After deciding to change my major to DMT, I did not regret the decision because it gave me a lot of opportunities and experiences and I got to meet new professors and staff through CIT. For the first time we took a CIT trip to Chicago to become involved in the International Manufacturing Technology Show IMTS

Harmony of Expressions

Fair 2022! This was like reliving my freshman year again but only at a higher level. However this was a tough semester and school year returning to UM-Flint because not only did I fall back in the hole of financial debt, I began to struggle looking for employment on campus.

    A month later in October, my mother caught COVID-19 again, and this time I was very worried about her because I was away from home and I could not lose my mother from COVID-19! My anxiety began to swell and I prayed and prayed even harder for her to recover and receive another chance…Thankfully in a week's time she recovered, and I couldn't be more grateful than ever because I was beyond grateful! Visiting home was more difficult for me because during the pandemic my public transportation business - Greyhound in my hometown closed for good when the pandemic hit making it extremely hard to others to commute from Muskegon to other places…Overall the pandemic and quarantine experience was like a reversal of college adaptation to home. It was like going from losing my grandfather to graduating high school and going off to college to losing my grandmother to going off to college and getting sucked back to home from the COVID-19 pandemic outbreak and now back to college. Basically it was like going from 2017 to 2019 to back to 2016 because I was still in high school in 2016 and taking those online courses at home from college felt like I was back in high school as if I was taking online classes from high school like the rest of the students.

Kirks

2021 was the peak of this horrible situation because that was when things began to escalade and become worse and caused breaking points from many people. But 2020 took the cake after 2019 ended, 2021 had put the icing on the cake and 2022 added the sprinkles and cherry on the cake. 2023 is where the cake is getting taken back and given to us all and we could finally eat our cake in 2023 and 2024 plus more!

I am now officially a senior and I have been accepted in the King-Chavez-Parks at the University of Michigan-Flint in the Fall of 2023 and I must say that 2023 has been the year that things began to fall in place in spite of the mild pandemic. Health restrictions were lifted in May, I have begun finding employment and have also begun working on campus and outside of college and I've also started my first internship in the Summer of 2023 returning to Shape Corporation and have returned back to college with high financial stability! I've decided that it's really time for me to hit the ground running with my last semesters and leave another mark at the University of Michigan-Flint filled with memories and legacies.

My biggest takeaway from this new decade is taking new opportunities and enjoying life while you can because once again tomorrow is never promised to anyone. Try new things and adapt to new experiences because you never know what cup of tea is yours until you keep sipping and also know that sometimes you have to take two steps back to spring five steps forward!

A Personal Essay

Icarus Jones

Harmony of Expressions

Twice in my college career, I have been given a test meant to highlight my personal values or what is most important to me, and both times art/self-expression has been my top value. I have learned that if you ask strangers what they believe is most important in their career you may get answers like salary, respect, recognition, work-life balance, promotions, etc. The most important part of any career to me is passion. When I was in my second year of college I had yet another semester with my favorite theater teacher, Janet Haley who told my class that if you do what you love the money will follow. That moment made me reevaluate my life and future. What did I really want to do? What would I do if money wasn't an issue? The answer I found was that I need a life full of passion. Like many people in the world I struggle with my mental health, I have bipolar disorder which is a continuous struggle in my life, a struggle that I offset by filling my life so full of what makes me happy that I have no choice but to stick around. Since I was diagnosed with bipolar in 2022 I have made it my mission to fill my life with things that make me happy, with things I am passionate about.

    I have since discovered two passions that I plan to make into a career, acting and glassblowing. I come from a long line of actors from my great-great- great grandfather Frank "Peg-Leg" Jones who was a one legged tap dancer and actor to my father who has been in movies like Ferris Buellers Day Off and Waynes World. I was in a few plays in middle school but it wasn't until college that I truly discovered my passion and talent for acting. I have been endlessly supported by my acting teacher and without her would never have had the courage to pursue the life I want. I have had the opportunity to act, improvise, and direct. I recently had a dream of mine come true and got to direct my first short play. For my short play I picked two scenes from a play I used to practice with my father when I was younger about a daughter losing her father and the final call between them as her father dies on a mountain. It is a very tragic play and I proudly brought tears to the audience.

My other career path I mentioned above is glass-blowing, I first discovered my love for glass blowing in 2023 at the Michigan Renaissance Festival. I have been going to the renaissance festival for my entire life but last year was the first year that I truly fell in love with it. There is a booth at the renaissance festival that has blown glass as well as live glass blowing demonstration which is what drew my attention. I passed by with my sister and was drawn in by a performer inviting us to the front row, I quickly took my place on the peeling purple benches and my life was changed forever. They were making the most beautiful goblet I have ever seen, a venetian style dragon stem goblet. Immediately I had fallen in love, I knew this glass had to be mine and that I wanted to learn how to make beautiful things like that one day. This quickly began a spiral into the world of glass blowing, I love everything to do with it. I began connecting with other glass blowers and taking lessons at the Flint Institute of Arts as well as Glass

Harmony of Expressions

Academy in Dearborn and my love has only grown deeper. I have taken two semesters of glass blowing classes so far and with every lesson I fall more in love. I have met so many amazing people and truly found my passion

A Personal Essay

Serentity Johnson

Harmony of Expressions

My experience up to this point has been pretty difficult. I'm not going to lie and paint a dream, but it has taught me a lot about life and being an adult. Don't get me wrong I have had a lot of fun times in my journey but some rough ones, but it all taught me lessons.

Now believe it or not U of M was not my first option, it wasn't even in my list. But one day I was talking to my advisor in high school about the type of career I would settle on which was business and she vouched for U of M. She showed me all this information about the college, its campus, and their business program. I also did some research on my own and decided that I'm going to go for it. I aced my interview with a promise scholar recruiter and my journey went from there.

The hardest part of my whole journey was leaving home. Anyone that has lived home with their parents for their whole life knows it's hard to leave that comfort. Of course I cried and was a little down when I first got to campus, but after some socializing and spending more time on campus and getting used to my new routine everything wasn't so bad.

Getting up and making it to classes was harder than I thought it would be since I woke up every morning for high school at 6 am I thought I could do it at 8 am. Rule number one I would give freshmen is don't do 8 a.m. or 9 a.m. unless you have to make that mistake once. Also it's very easy to skip your classes when your mom and dad aren't there to tell you to go. Once you miss one lecture you'll continue to find excuses to miss more, but you gotta remember you're paying for these classes not anyone else.

Being in college really teaches you how to really take care of yourself like grocery shopping, cleaning, cooking and staying on top of everything while trying to maintain some type of social life. The things that sounded so easy and simple become very difficult when you have to figure it out yourself. When I had to grocery shop for the first time by myself I was appalled at how hard it was. I didn't know what snacks to get, what meals to get and if I was going to eat them. I had a newfound respect for my parents.

Also if you plan to ever live on campus a big obstacle you'll have to face is roommates whether or not if you guys have the same interpretation of clean or if you can get along. But having roommates is truly an experience. It helps you see people who came from different backgrounds and how they operate in a 'home' setting. You're going to have arguments about dumb things and serious things, but you will get through it just teaches you to compromise. It's like having the sibling you never asked for.

Also a big thing I want to address is friends. In college especially friends will come and go. You might have this big friend group one day then next week you might not have it. Your best friend in the world today and not even talk to them the next month it happens. The important thing is to not dwell on it. We are in a part of our life when things are going to be changing rapidly everyday and it's normal. It's not like high school when you are all going down the same path. We are going to very dif-

Harmony of Expressions

ferent places we don't even know we're going to and sometimes that makes friends drift. But it's something that you have to accept and eventually move on and live your own life. Things may seem bad or it's too much one day, but the next you are going to be so happy you pulled through to see the next day.

In college you get tested in every shape and form. It's all in how you handle it and what support system you have around you. Don't be afraid to reach out and get help with anything you're dealing with because I promise you are not alone. For me knowing that there are other people who are dealing with the same problems I'm dealing with makes me feel more at peace with myself instead of being all in my emotions and feeling alone.

The Importance of Forgiveness

Meghan Johnson

Harmony of Expressions

Every individual is born into this world that is full of sin. Somewhere along our life journey, everyone encounters those individuals who make life worth living whereas others who make life impossible to deal with. They often say, kindness goes a long way, however, I'm starting to have my doubts about that because sometimes kindness isn't always enough for some people. Has there ever been a time in your life where you've had a hard time forgiving someone who mistreated you and didn't even bother to apologize? Even though you've been nothing but nice to them. Well, sad to say, I have experienced this.

Forgiveness to me is defined as making a decision to let go of any and all past or present situations that involve hurt and anger. Forgiveness to me is also basically a synonym of healing. In other words both healing and forgiveness take a significant amount of time. Like most people, forgiveness used to be really hard for me. I struggled with it really badly. Now that I'm able to reflect on my life in the past, I have come to the conclusion that I was one miserable individual. But then, God stepped in and gave me a chance to restructure my life and instructed me on how to handle heartbreak without sinning. I wasn't able to forgive until I got some kind of revenge. During this time of my life, I found myself dealing with a lot of hurt, shame and anger. I wanted to be freed from those feelings that didn't mean me any good. So, I decided to start my spiritual growth journey. This challenged me to read my bible more, pray more and it even allowed me to gain more patience. This was the time where I found myself being more tested than ever. However, I stuck to God's word and I made it through. I felt content about my growth and life circumstances. I learned that revenge isn't my responsibility, it's Gods.

Just a couple of years ago, I experienced heartbreak in a friendship again and I decided to handle it in a different way. I made a decision to put the situation, my feelings and my thoughts into God's hands. Instead of seeking revenge, I decided to pray about it and forgive that individual immediately instead of letting the hurt linger. As a therapeutic treatment, I decided to write a letter and burn it. Just a few weeks ago, I encountered that individual and greeted them with love like nothing ever happened. Later on that night, I thought about the old me and how ugly that situation could have escalated had I not forgiven that individual.

Having Christ doesn't change what you go through, it changes how you go through it. I realized that if I had not forgiven that person, I wouldn't be where I am today. Forgiveness keeps you grounded, on track, allows you to grow, allows you to persevere and most of all it doesn't require or mean reconnection. It just means that you are free from all the hurt that tries to keep you down. Forgiveness grants you access to deliverance and allows you to walk into your abundance. Forgiveness is not for the other person, it's for you.

The Impact of Unemployment Benefits

Mariah James

Harmony of Expressions

The purpose of unemployment checks is to help individuals that have lost their jobs and are actively trying to find work to help with expenses at home. However, unemployment checks are becoming more popular throughout the United States with unemployment being at 3.9% in October 2023 and last year the unemployment rate being 3.4 in October 2022. This paper investigates the reason why it's so hard to get off unemployment after being unemployed for a long period of time. To answer this research question I used quantitative research to help me figure out why unemployment has been a big primary source of income instead of trying to keep finding jobs. My results demonstrate that being on unemployment can help individuals for a certain amount of time until the unemployment checks run out but after a while it's going to be time for you to really get up and try finding a new job. In conclusion, unemployment is a very helpful source to use once I have lost my job or I voluntarily leave my job but, It gives me a chance to relax for a couple months to get my life back on track and find a job that suits me better .

Keywords: jobless, inactive, underemployed

James

Unemployment Taking Over

In 2020, global unemployment reached its highest level due to the pandemic (Civilian unemployment rate (n.d.). Covid-19 caused so many people to lose their jobs due to the fact that so many businesses closed or reduced staff due to the lockdowns.

Unemployment benefits are a form of a payment given to a person that has lost their jobs due to many reasons. Wisconsin was one of the first states in the United States to pass the first public unemployment insurance program. Wisconsin offered 50% of wage compensation for a maximum of 10 weeks funded through a payroll tax imposed on employers. Which was a pleasant thing for those people without jobs but their unemployment benefits were a maximum of 10 weeks so they gave those individuals time to find a new job.

In order for you to receive unemployment benefits individuals must go through the application process which can take up to two weeks for the benefits to start. Individuals can disqualify or be denied for unemployment benefits. You do in fact have a right to appeal if you agree with the decision. If you voluntarily quit your job you must prove that it was for a good reason. If not, that's another reason you can be denied unemployment benefits. What is the correlation between gender and unemployment rates in Michigan? In Michigan you can only get 20 weeks of unemployment with each week you can only get 362 dollars and you get paid biweekly. Also in Michigan to qualify for unemployment you must actively be looking for jobs, must be unemployed, and you must have earned a certain amount of wages during a specific time period. You are likely ineligible for benefits if you were fired for failing a drug test, stealing property, assaulting someone or even not showing up without your employer being notified.

Unemployment inequality happens when joblessness hits harder for some individuals who don't have a functional lifestyle. Conflict theory ties in a lot with unemployment where societal resources aren't equally distributed. Unemployment is a result of social inequalities due to the fact that those with more power or resources often have better job security, while those with less may face higher employment rates. You also wouldn't qualify for receiving unemployment benefits if you voluntarily quit your job. Unemployment can be seen as a negative situation but also leads to positive outcomes for individuals. It helps provide opportunities for people to reassess their career goals and explore new paths for themselves.

On a personal level being unemployed can sometimes offer a much needed break for people who have been in high stress jobs and it also provides more time for people to spend with their families or engage in activities they enjoy. Race and gender can influence unemployment due to societal biases and discrimination *(Farber & Valletta, 2015)*. It's a very big sociological issue because it's about how society and its structures can impact people 's life and opportunities by getting unemployment.

There wouldn't need to be unemployment given out so much if there were more job opportunities, providing support to find jobs, and providing the people with skill development. You can make the best out of unemployment by getting involved in your community, building new friendships, and making time for fun. It is more fitting for individuals who have a smaller social network because the relationships are more intimate and you can also build stronger bonds which makes everyone feel more important *(Wood, 2013)*.

One important reason people are unemployed is because they are laid off from their job due to the lack of work , lack of funds, and because of reorganization. Unemployment is a complex issue with economic and psychological impacts. It's not about joblessness, but also about societal factors like race, gender, and biases. The stress of unemployment can affect mental health, leading to anxiety and hopelessness. It's an economic concern too, causing reduced spending and slower growth. Eligibility for benefits varies, adding another layer of complexity. Addressing unemployment requires creating job opportunities, offering support for job seekers, and implementing policies for economic stability. It's a multifaceted issue needing a comprehensive approach.

Understanding these aspects can help in formulating effective strategies to combat unemployment. "As many as 46 million individuals received unemployment benefits in 2020" *(GWYN, 2022)*.

Harmony of Expressions

That helped a lot of individuals put food on the table for their families and bills they couldn't pay at the moment. During the pandemic so many individuals had to try to find jobs and some type of work to keep money coming into their homes with the unemployment benefits being so limited. "Short and long-term effects of unemployment on health behaviors such as smoking, drinking, and body weight have yielded mixed results" *(Bolton & Rodriguez, 2009)*. I believe this is somewhat true due to the fact that some individuals get unemployment benefits and waste it on things like drugs and alcohol. There should be a current type of way individuals should be able to use their benefits.

The government isn't giving people benefits to waste it on things that aren't needed. The government benefits shouldn't be abused, it should be used to pay a bill, get food for their families, or even try saving a little amount of money. There are some individuals who take advantage of the system because they don't necessarily need them but, I believe the system is more worried about helping the people in need of the benefits in using them appropriately helping the people in need of the benefits in using them appropriately helping those individuals who take advantage of the system. Women with children often face more barriers to employment which can result in higher reliance on government benefits *(Holster, Hubbard & Strain, 2023)*.

In my opinion this is due to the lack of child care because it's an important factor for instability for low income mothers with young children. Another thing is mothers with children that have any type of disabilities of some sort. So the physical disabilities of the child can or may affect the parent being able to work so it calls in unemployment benefits so the mother can get help to take care of her child til she can be able to figure something out.

Unemployment benefits have both quantitative and qualitative data due to the fact it's quantitative because I looked at bar graphs to see when unemployment benefits increased in the past 10 years. Also quantitative because it helps understand why and how individuals help get on unemployment benefits. Unemployment benefits can be quantitative in several different ways with all different ways providing many different perspectives on the impact.

One of the main factors is the total number of individuals receiving benefits which I looked at a bar graph *(Civilian unemployment rate (n.d.)*. Which showed how many people are currently relying on government support due to joblessness.

The second thing I looked at was the total amount of money getting distributed through the unemployment benefits. I looked into the amount of money due the fact it represents the financial cost of the program to the government and to the taxpayers. The benefits are another duration of quantifiable aspect. Some individuals might receive benefits for a few weeks while others might receive them for several months. It just depends on people's circumstances. My last quantitative research was looking at the percentage of the unemployed population that already receives the benefits because not all individ-

Harmony of Expressions

uals that are unemployed get the benefits because not all individuals that are unemployed get the benefits. So It helped me to see how accessible and effective the benefits system is.

Unemployment benefits are also qualitative because they offer more than financial help. They provide a benefit that can help support mental health and also reduce stress during the tough times of not having a job. Also with the benefits it gives individuals time to find a job that better suits their interest. Qualitative data looks more into the personal experiences and the impact of unemployment. So I talked to my 21 year old cousin about his experience of being fired from his job working at a factory and being unemployed for 6 months. I asked questions like how often did he get paid, how much was he getting paid, and what did he used to get benefits for. He said "I got the benefits every two weeks, my benefits were 568.62 and I used the money for essentials like gas, food, and clothing when needed" After the talk with him I realized he still lives with his parents so he doesn't have to worry about paying any bills so, that's a decent amount of money coming in for him while he looks for a new job. This quali]tive data helped me understand the side of unemployment benefits and the effects hearing it from someone I knew personally. It's about the experiences behind the quantitative data. In conclusion, unemployment benefits are a wonderful thing the government is doing. Now there are people that receive the benefits that don't really need them.

James

Researching unemployment benefits made me realize that it had a lot to do with sociology. Conflict theory was a major factor because the benefits can cause conflict between the interests of the working class and the interests of the business class. I feel like it causes conflict because there are people working hard for their money to pay their bills. Then, there are people that are getting money for losing their jobs. I feel like what the government is doing for individuals is such a wonderful thing. The benefits give those people who lost their jobs a chance to find a job that they can really enjoy.

Unemployment benefits play a crucial role in society. It helps provide a life worth living during the times of joblessness. Gender does not really have a lot to do with the benefit due to the fact that most people think that men get more benefits then women but that's not the case. The amount of unemployment benefits depends on their previous earnings, not their gender. Unemployment benefits definitely should be researched and talked about more so those individuals can get more help finding jobs so others can get on the unemployment and it could just be a cycle. Doing research on this made me realize that there's a lot of things that are pushed under the rug. If people talk about the unemployment rates more I believe It would have an impact on helping figure out why the hiring process takes so long.

References

Bolton, K. L., & Rodriguez, E. (2009). Smoking, drinking and body weight after re-employment: does unemployment experience and compensation make a difference? BMC Public Health, 9(1), 77–77. https://doi.org/10.1186/1471-2458-9-77

Farber, H. S., & Valletta, R. G. (2015). Do Extended Unemployment Benefits Lengthen Unemployment Spells? Evidence from Recent Cycles in the U.S. Labor Market. The Journal of Human Resources, 50(4), 873–909. https://doi.org/10.3368/jhr.50.4.873

GWYN, N (2022, March 24). Historic unemployment programs provided vital support to workers and the economy during pandemic, offer roadmap for future reform. https://www.cbpp.org/research/economy/historic-unemployment-programs-provided-vital-support-to-workers-and-the-economy

MORALES-SUÁREZ-VARELA, M., KAERLEV, L., ZHU, J. L., BONDE, J. P., NOHR, E. A., LLOPIS-GONZÁLEZ, A., GIMENO-CLEMENTE, N., & OLSEN, J. (2011). Unemployment and pregnancy outcomes: A study within the Danish National Birth Cohort. Scandinavian Journal of Public Health, 39(5), 449–456. https://doi.org/10.1177/1403494811407672

Wood, E. (2013, January 09). Why be active in small

social networks. Crowd Content Blog. 20small%20 networks%2C%20the%20relationships,to%20 build%20on%20larger%20platforms.https://www. crowdcontent.com/blog/social-media/why-be-active-in-small-social-networks/#:~:text=Small%20 Social%20Networks%20%3D%20Less%20Competition&text=In%

U.S Bureau of Labor Statistics. (n.d.). Civilian unemployment rate. https://www.bls.gov/charts/employment-situation/civilian-unemployment-rate.htm

A Personal Essay

Gus Ivanac

Harmony of Expressions

When I first came to college it was really difficult for me as I did not know anybody on campus and the pandemic was still going on at this time which made it harder to socialize with other students and caused me to just be in my room for the majority of the day. I made it so that I was lonely and this combined with the fact that this was my first time living away from home and had almost nothing to distract me from this. With all this going on I fell into a depression, everyday I thought "I just gotta get through it." I had trouble eating and even sleeping. The parts of my school year that were somewhat enjoyable were the walks I went on as they always felt like I was away from my problems and my frequent weekend visits to home as it was when I felt like I was back home.

With these problems my first year at college was awful, as much as I tried to convince myself it was not, it was, and so it comes as no surprise that I was afraid going into my second year of college as I was afraid that it would be just as bad. For about the first week of the semester I was still stressed out and worried about the year being awful again that I did not even realize that it really was not anywhere near as bad. I was so caught up on how bad my first year was that I almost let it ruin my second year too. Luckily I realized that now I have been away from home before and there was no more mystery on what that was like and in addition to that the pandemic was not nearly as bad by that point so there was a lot less reasons for me to be worried and whenever I started to feel down I would just remind myself of this and kept going. With this thought process I was able to make a lot of friends, join some student organizations and actually start to enjoy my life on campus. It got to the point where I was not just okay with being on campus, I really liked it and started not needing to go home for the weekend as frequently because I loved to be at school. After a while I started to not even think about the possibility that going back to college would cause me to feel anxious or upset. It was a hard transition for me but in the end it was really just a matter of keeping a positive outlook and not focusing on all the bad stuff that happened in the past, with this in mind I was able to make myself more comfortable at college, and after that I started doing things that made it so that I liked being at college. The most important thing to keep in mind in situations like this is that it always gets better.

On To the Next Station

Chris Hartman

Harmony of Expressions

College, much like a train, has gone steadily down the tracks for me. When I finished my very first year in April of 2021, life was much different then. COVID-19 was still prevalent in our daily lives, and social interaction wasn't very common on campus. With an unknown of what to expect come the fall, I went home, ready and eager for fall to come. I could never have predicted how the next three years would have gone, and just how much I would grow to love school.

Entering my sophomore year, I met my first on-campus friends, and began to form strong bonds that continue to this day. I saw more and more events happening, and I started to see the campus life I expected. The school year of 2021-2022 was not only where I started to get the real college experience, but where I formed some crucial friendships that I value to this day. I also finally chose my major, and decided what path I wanted to go down for my degree. I had battled in my head whether I wanted to pursue a degree in the arts, but looking back on it, I am happy I went down this path. I checked off another year in my mind, amazed that I was already halfway done.

During the summer of 2022, and looking towards my junior year, now with some idea of where I wanted to go career wise, I was extremely excited for the year to come. I had applied for an on-campus job, and little did I know that getting that job would change everything for me when it came to my friends. I had met my group through a coworker of mine, who then introduced me to his friends, and so on, and as of now I have quite a large circle. This school year was full of fun, happiness, sadness, all the emotions you could think of, and more. I found a confidence in myself and my decisions I didn't have before. I look back extremely fondly to this year, as it also helped prepare me for the next stop on my track of life; the final year of college.

The school year of 2023-2024 was extremely bittersweet for me, as I prepared for life beyond school, and tried to enjoy the most with the friends who were graduating that year. Coming home from school, it's shockingly difficult to adjust to not seeing your best friends every day, or as often as you did. You don't realize just how much whiplash your routine changing gives you. Despite the challenges that came with a more difficult course load, and more difficult problems, I finished it as I have done all four years, I did it well.

And so, we come to the final stop of my college experience, the summer before my last semester. While I am very frightened of what comes next, and having to do real adult stuff, I can't help but be satisfied with my college experience. When I think of me and all my friends going separate ways, it's extremely sad, but it also makes me grateful for all the opportunities I did have with them. The biggest piece of advice I can give anyone starting this journey is to take every opportunity you can while you're here!

One part time job led to me forming some of my closest bonds. Who knows what could happen if you make a split second decision. The college experience is truly a rollercoaster; it goes a lot faster than you'd

Harmony of Expressions

expect, but I believe I am now ready to get onto the next station of lif; graduation and beyond.

Regretting

An Anonymous Writer

Harmony of Expressions

In this poignant short story, a teenage girl named Star navigates the complexities of family dynamics, divorce, and loss. Through Star's introspective narrative, we witness her struggles with self-image, strained relationships, and the gradual unraveling of her family's stability. The story delves into her emotional journey as she copes with her beloved Nana's sudden illness, leading to a coma and eventual passing. Star grapples with guilt, grief, and questions of faith as she confronts the harsh realities of mortality and the fragility of familial bonds. Through vivid imagery and raw honesty, the story explores themes of resilience, love, and the profound impact of loss on a young soul. This story isn't a happy ending and is meant for you to take out of it, only of what you need.

"It couldn't," I thought. "This couldn't be happening." "Not to her, not to me." I felt horribly guilty.

The faces in front of me blurred, and every sound around turned to white noise—the arguing of my cousins, the sounds of soup cooking on the stove, the rain outside. I tried to contain the feeling that slowly developed through me, but I couldn't help it. After one tear fell down my cheek, they all began to roll. Despite the comfort of my parents' arms (who were no longer together), I continued to cry.

***

Harmony of Expressions

"Just smile," Nana said, snapping multiple photos of me and my cousin Sam. It was freshman year, and we had both decided to show our faces at the Homecoming Dance. Sam stepped out in a blue fluffy skirt and a short top with silver heels to match. Everyone came out to see us off—our shared grandmother, my grandmother on my dad's side, and both our moms.

I was 14 going on 15 at the time, a growing teenager developing character, likes, dislikes, and more. For me, I didn't like pictures. No, I hated pictures because I never felt like I looked right in them. It was a struggle with my arms and face, and I would end up looking ridiculous—just as I did on the day of homecoming. I searched high and low for dresses, but stores never accommodated big women. The only decent thing I found was a black jumpsuit with a long sheer cape flowing from my hip line. I didn't like it, but I didn't want to miss my first homecoming.

"Hey, twin," my cousin called out, and I turned around. "We should take a picture like this." She crouched down, sticking one leg out and one leg in for support, and I obliged. After we finished taking pictures, we prepared to leave.

"Aw, my chocolate princess is going to the homecoming," Lynette said.

"Ugh, Mom," I exclaimed, rolling my eyes and scooting away, hoping she'd stop, but the same came from my grandmother's mouth.

"My Moody Judy," my grandmother said.

"Moody Judy" was a nickname everyone practically called me on my father's side because I'm not

Harmony of Expressions

much of the smiling, lovely, all-around family member type. I didn't like to smile. It wasn't easy to find reasons to smile, especially with my parents going through a horrible divorce, and me just starting high school. My grandmother often touched me in ways I didn't like, smacking me on the butt or commenting on my weight. Although I hated it then, I would do anything for it now.

"All right, all right, where's Tina?"

"Yeah, where's my mom?" said Sam. As soon as we finished our sentences, Tina rushed out of the house to wish us all goodbye.

Days passed after homecoming, and life went on like normal. Every Sunday at six o'clock, I switched from one parent to the other. My parents co-parented, alternating weeks to spend time with us. This week happened to be my dad's. While my dad still lived in the house we purchased before the breakup, my mom didn't. In fact, she didn't even have her own place. We lived with our grandmother, along with nine other people, in a two-bedroom house. Some of us stayed upstairs, some in the basement. It was fun for my brother, but I knew the gravity of the situation. We had been living there for about a year and a half, maybe even two. I wanted to be able to enjoy it- staying with my cousins, but I didn't. For a teenager I was going through a lot at the moment.

Who could possibly deal with the immediate split of their parents, feeling isolated at school, feeling like black sheep at home, and struggling with self love and image at the same time .Sometimes this led me to being extremely irritable, but could you

Harmony of Expressions

blame me.

I got a text from my dad saying that he was outside. Because my parents didn't talk, my brother and I walked outside and got into the car.

We drove around the corner to my Nana's house. It was weird. It was October, so usually, there were decorations outside, but there was nothing. My grandmother was an adamant decorator, and every holiday was met with elaborate decor inside and out. Instead, I stared at the blank porch. We got out of the car and knocked on the door.

"Hey, Tay," she said, looking at my father. "Hey, Moody Judy."

"Hey," I replied.

"I called you, and you didn't even answer the phone," she said, stepping outside to sit on the porch. We didn't go inside because my dad and my papa didn't talk anymore, for almost four years now, maybe more.

I looked at my phone, and she was right. She did call me, but I rarely talked to people on the phone—I just didn't want to. It was one of those early teenage quirks, I guess. While sitting there, you could tell that she didn't look okay. She already had diabetes and had just had her toe amputated. She always talked about feeling ill, but I never thought much of it because she always got over it. My Nana was surprisingly strong. She always stood up for herself. She didn't take crap and that's what I felt like I wasn't capable of doing- saying no. I loved my nana. She has always been there for me since day one. She sparked my love for reading, for my education,

Harmony of Expressions

and more. A lot of the good times of my life involve memories of me with her. Her job was to protect me, to love me. Those feelings never strayed.

As much as it hurt me mentally and emotionally I never felt capable of saying no or even sharing my opinions to my family. I felt dismissed, especially in times of need.

My nana talked to Tj for a while, going on and on about work and friends, as always. It eventually got late, and we went on our way back to the house.

***

"You need to start answering people's calls, Star .," my dad said, his tone not very happy. In all honesty, he never sounded happy. I didn't really think he liked me all that much, but perhaps it was the pain of the ongoing divorce. Maybe I reminded him too much of mother.

Maybe I just wasn't good enough, period. I struggled with these thoughts constantly, never feeling good enough, never perfect enough, never pretty enough. So most of my time was spent buried in books and school, and guy friends to distract myself from the intimacy I felt I lacked from my family.

He continued... "You never know when it's going to be the last time you talk to someone. Your phone is always on silent, that's why you can't hear anyone calling you... it's like you're hiding something."

While he talked, I sat and listened. I was used to the constant talks—I learned that it was better off if I didn't say anything. I didn't feel understood or

Harmony of Expressions

heard; I didn't understand what I was doing wrong all the time. It felt like every move I made was wrong enough to get me yelled at.

***

Halloween was soon approaching, and I figured I was getting too old to dress up. In Walmart, they sold these animal heads that everyone was into, so I decided to buy one of those. My papa's birthday was also coming up, and my dad decided to buy him something. Another week passed with my mom, and I was back with my dad again. Sometimes I just didn't get them—they were always arguing about each other to me but didn't understand the position they were putting me in. It was awkward. No child wants to be the middleman of two grown adults fighting, especially not your parents. What am I supposed to say back? Maybe the truth I always thought.

Like routine, we again went over to my Nana's, but it was now my papa's birthday. Once we walked up to the house, he was already outside. It felt so awkward. I looked at my dad, then at my papa, waiting to see who would talk.

"How have you been?" Bruce started off, trying to break the thick ice between them.

"I've been good. Busy with work and these two over here," my father replied.

My dad walked towards him and handed him a gift card to Halo Burger. It wasn't much, but it was enough to get him excited. My papa loved Halo

Harmony of Expressions

Burger. We spent the rest of the day finally inside the house together, talking about the plans for the night. This moment slightly relieved the uncomfortable tension I felt constantly.

"BYE, GRANDBABY!" my papa shouted across the living room. I walked up to Nana, gave her a hug, and told her I would see her later. I didn't know I was lying when I said that. Something told me I needed to give her a hug, call it a higher power or gut instinct, but I knew I had to despite my dislike for physical touch.

Another week passed, and I was now with my mom. Life seemed impossible at the time—I had to deal with school, my parents' divorce, and living with a horde of people. The world couldn't have been more against me. It was cold and raining outside, and once again, I was getting my fifth lecture of the week. My grandma and mother always yelled at me for any little thing.

"Just go!" my grandmother yelled. "Just go back up the stairs and be lazy like you always are. We don't need your help." It was over soup. Because I didnt want to make soup. I was the only person in the house that cared about my career or education. All of the 9 people in that house and none of them went to college or had any plans of college, shitty jobs, and no morals and goals. I didn't want to be like them. I wanted to be better. So I worked and worked.. I just wanted a break that's all, and for that I was often considered cold, and uncaring. I stormed up to my room to calm down and get ready—I had to go to dance anyway. From all the madness, I

Harmony of Expressions

found a way to slip into a deep sleep.

"Star ... Star ..." I jumped up after feeling a push on my arm. It was my other cousin, Brianna. "Your dad is downstairs," she said.

My dad? What possible reason could my dad have for being downstairs? I hadn't called him, and it wasn't Sunday. I rolled to the far side of the bed and began my walk to the steps. I walked down the steps in the living room and past the kitchen to reach the door. Once I was at the door, my mother was standing there too. Weird. Was I in trouble?

"Well, Star," my dad began. "Some people have health problems, and sometimes those issues can cause things like a stroke. Some people die from strokes, some people get better." He paused for a while, looking at me. "Well, your Nana had one, and now she's in a coma..."

Fades, Soup, Arguing, Rain
I cried for about 30 minutes in front of my parents, for the first time I can remember. It didn't get better after that. I stopped eating as much, I didn't really talk at school, I had constant mood swings, but I still made sure I did what needed to be done in school. For many months, my Nana lay in the hospital bed. I was scared to touch her—I didn't know what would happen if I did. Would I hurt her? Would she feel it? My aunt told so many stories about how she blinked or moved her head, and even squeezed her hand. One day, I was brave enough to walk up to her. I looked and stared at her for a while. I always thought she might be somewhere fighting her way back through literal obstacles. I had enough courage

Harmony of Expressions

to take my hand and place it on hers.

I whispered in her ear, "Hey. It's Moody Judy… Can you squeeze my hand, please…"

Nothing happened. Maybe she didn't hear me. This time, I rubbed my thumb over the top of her hand, but she wouldn't budge. Her hand was cold and stiff, like she was already pronounced dead. I had dreams about her waking up, and I hoped she did, but God had done this to her, so maybe he was punishing me by ripping the only family away from me(at least emotionally). Or maybe there wasn't one. I prayed. I really did. I even went to the pastor and prayed with him forever. But he didn't hear us. He turned his back on me. So I did too.

After a couple of months had passed, my Nana was constantly being transferred to different hospitals, and they didn't know how to wake her up. By the looks of it, they weren't doing anything for her; it looked more like they were hurting her than helping her. After multiple trips from the hospital and back, we went as much as we could.

Seven months had passed, and I started to feel a lot better than before. I don't think I ever properly dealt with the introduction to her coma. I buried myself in books because that's what I was taught to do, focus on school. I wasn't really able to express much of my emotions either, as I had no friends to converse with, no relationship with my family, and no privacy or independence as a growing teenager to grief or think or process. So with my methods, I was fine..until I got another phone call. It was my dad; I answered.

Harmony of Expressions

Before I could say hello, he told me, "I have some bad news. Your Nana just passed."

I stared. I couldn't move. I couldn't feel anything for a while until I dropped my phone completely and began to sob out loud.

"Star, what's wrong?" my mother asked, but I ignored her.

"Star!" She ran up to me, picked up my phone, and hugged me. After that, my faith left my body, or maybe just a little faith that I had left. If there really was a God, why would he take her away from me like that? Was he punishing me? I wish I would have answered her calls. Why'd I have to be such a terrible granddaughter? All that time I was looking for someone to care for and it was her that cared and I took that for granted. After a while, my mom must have invited my grandmother and my grandpa over and told him what happened because he sat there with me the rest of the night until I fell asleep.

When my mother's week was over, I went back to my dad. The entire week we didn't talk about her; he didn't mention her. The only thing we said was when the funeral was that Saturday. Friday night before the funeral, I wrote a poem. It wasn't good, but I wrote what I felt. It read...

That paper
That obituary, that thing
It reminds me off to much
So much
The words Sunset and sunrise made me hate it
Makes me hate myself.
All the calls I missed.

Harmony of Expressions

I could've heard her voice.
Ever since I remember, she's been there.
A room just for me
Hot, sweating days, and cold dark nights spent at her house.
My name plastered above the foot of the door in green and white letters.
Flying silver butterflies, and more pink and dora you could ever imagine. When mornings came she always cooked
That doesn't mean she was good at it.
she had a thing for decoration and dressing.
In her home the bathrooms would always be some kind of character.
Mickey, or even Spongebob.
Colorful things everywhere filled the house.
Holidays were crazy wild
Halloween was my favorite
It always consists of standing at the porch
music playing in our ears
filling children with fear from her costumes.
When I grew up always remembered her working at a school.
In the library of course because we both loved books.
We sat in the library
read books and talked and laughed and always had fun.
As I got older she began calling me mood judy
I hated the name but it was mine and mine to keep.
She was always there for me,
every performance, recital, meeting, she was there

Harmony of Expressions

I thought it would always be like that.

Black Lives Matter
Tamaria Garrett

Harmony of Expressions

In streets where cries resound,
Something starts to move, very high.
A firm call in hearts ablaze,
For equality and justice for all.
Joining voices, they stand for dignity throughout the nation.
It is unavoidably true that Black lives matter in all hues and shades. Despite overcoming obstacles and triumphing in conflicts, their journey is far from over. Even on the darkest nights, they find strength in solidarity every hour of the day. Their voices are heard, their strength remains, for rights denied and dreams postponed. Black lives matter is a timeless message that appears in every rhyme and phrase. Thus, let us take a stand and join forces in the struggle of solidarity.
Black lives matter for justice, peace, and liberty forever.

A Person Essay

Kaitlyn Franz

Harmony of Expressions

At the start of the pandemic, I applied for the University of Michigan-Flint. I did this in my aunt's basement with the hope that sometime soon things would go back to normal. It ended up taking a lot longer than I think any of us initially expected, but making the decision to go to college during this time was one of the smartest decisions I made during this time. Although celebrate all you have accomplished while you were in high school and don't rush college too fast because they are vastly different. I ended up starting at the University of Michigan-Flint back in 2020 during the middle of the pandemic.

    I was pretty nervous because I am a first generation college student and I was stuck at home because at the time the university was closed for any in-person events. There was a lot of uncertainty back then about what the future would look like, but there were always people at the University I could reach out to even during the middle of the pandemic. My biggest advice to freshman students is to attend your classes, talk to your peers and professors and never be afraid to reach out to people here. I spent three years doing online classes and during that time I forgot how important it really is to be around and talk to your peers. Another piece of advice that I had to learn during my college experience is to find someone or a small group of people who have the same major as you. I found this to be incredibly helpful because you are able to talk about the classes that you're taking and the classes in the future and the past and that person or group of people have also had to take those same classes to an extent. I found this to be incredibly helpful because then when you're having a hard time in a class you can message that person or group of people and discuss it. You can also learn different things about your major's expectations from this small group of people or person.

Another piece of advice that I would have for freshman students in particular but students in general is to not be scared that you can't do it. When I first chose to be an education major and become a teacher I was very nervous that I wouldn't be able to do it. I thought that it would be too hard, but now I am in my last semester as an undergraduate here and I am proud to say I did it, slowly but surely I completed all the requirements and I will be walking across the stage this upcoming December. Overall, I would say to enjoy your time in college because just as the four years in high school go by fast the four years in college goes by even faster. The important thing to remember is to enjoy your time and make friends. Go Michigan, Go Blue!

A Personal Essay

Andrea Fischer

Harmony of Expressions

In highschool, I struggled a bit to keep my grades up. I was a two sport athlete and I found it very difficult to succeed academically and athletically. I definitely cared more about my performance in sports than school, and I let my GPA slip. During COVID-19 especially, I had no motivation to focus on my schoolwork since all of it was online. My senior year of highschool I was finally able to go back in person, but my study habits were inconsistent and I struggled a lot. Everyone was choosing where they wanted to attend college, and I had no idea where I was going to go and who would accept me with my GPA. I was basically stuck and I knew nothing except one thing, I wanted to pursue a career in nursing.

My entire highschool career consisted of everyone telling me that I couldn't do it. Apparently my GPA and SAT results proved that I could not handle college, especially nursing, one of the hardest majors there is. My highschool advisors encouraged me to take the trade school route, and gave me the "not everyone has to go to college" speech countless times even when they knew how badly I wanted to go. I remember the instance very vividly when I told my biology teacher that I wanted to go into nursing, and she laughed at me. The narrative in highschool is that if you can't do well here, you won't do well there, and that's simply not true.

When I heard about the promise scholar program (now the KCP program) I did a lot of research into it. I did an interview, applied to the University, and got accepted through the program. I was extremely hesitant to go to college, especially since I had to dorm my first two years. But let me tell you, I am so glad I found this program. I remember being so lost and stuck in my senior year, and my confidence was so low, but I've made it to where I am now and I couldn't have done it without the help of everyone in this program. I knew that this was my only shot at college, and I definitely changed a lot of things like my study habits and attitude towards school.

    I am now an incoming junior and have completed pretty much all of my prerequisites and am currently waiting on my acceptance letter for nursing school this fall. My GPA is good standing, and I've worked very hard to maintain it. I also play basketball here, and I found a way to set my priorities straight between school, work, sports, and my social life. I understand now that school is my top priority, and everything else comes later. Me two years ago would be absolutely shocked to see how far I have come today. These last two years have been the best years of my life, and I cannot wait to graduate nursing school and prove everyone that told me that I couldn't do it, that I can, and I did. I will end this personal essay with a thank you to everyone in this program that helped me get to where I am today.

A Personal Essay

Zoe Doss

Harmony of Expressions

Covid-19 had a big impact on people's lives, for me I felt as if it had a bigger impact because I am immunocompromised. I was scared to get covid because I did not have a strong immune system. Even when we were not shut down and just had to wear masks I was still nervous to go out and be around people. Once we went back to school, I was a junior in high school and junior year was hard enough without covid. I struggled a lot in school during this time because I was so anxious about being at school. We had a lot of huge outbreaks of covid and would be virtual for 2 weeks or even more. I would get so anxious and have panic attacks because of the switching back and forth, as well as a lot of my friends would test positive so that did not help.

When our school first brought up going fully online, I did not want that as the year prior I had switched schools and did not get a lot of time to make new friends. At the end of the first semester, I had talked to my mom about going fully online as I was so anxious and my grades would increase when I was online. My moms both talked about it and agreed that I would do better online. I made sure that it was the right thing to do for my education. My school did an informational meeting to let us know what being online meant for us. We had an alternative program at our school, I thought they would just use the same site for the online students. They had told us that if we continued online that we would be enrolled in Michigan virtual school. My mom thought that it would help with my anxiety and keep me safe even though my step-siblings were still going in person. They knew how I was and still am in school and believed that I was the only one that would be successful in online school. I made a schedule for myself to complete the classes. I still wanted to be in band class because it was a place that I felt safe and it had become my second home. The school worked it out with me to be able to continue that class in person while the rest of my classes were online. I had done a lot better that semester because I was not so anxious about covid and was able to focus on my classes instead of being in an anxious state all the time.

The classes in Michigan Virtual were a lot different than any online class that I have taken in college. They opened all our assignments for a month out because we could work as far ahead as we would like up to a month. I was getting through all the learning and assignments for all my classes in two days. I would start to work on the next week's learning and assignments, due to this I was able to finish my junior year two weeks before the deadline and was able to start my summer break before everyone else. I got very good grades in my classes and did a lot better online then I did when I was in person. I did miss all the friends that were in person, because I was the only one of my friends that did online school.

Due to how covid had affected my school, juniors did not get to have a prom. That was pretty upsetting to me because that is what I was looking forward to all year. My moms were in the middle

Harmony of Expressions

of redoing our deck and decided to surprise my friends and the guy I was dating at the time. He was a senior at my old high school and did not want to go to prom if I was not allowed to go because we went to different schools. My mom was not going to let that happen and decorated the deck and had us invite over our friends who were not going to prom. She had made a prom for us at home and it was one of the highlights of my year. I think that covid did affect a lot but I do not think that I would have enjoyed prom as much as I did when my mom threw it for us. I think that if my school allowed juniors to go that I would have been too anxious to go or would have ruined it. I think that being chronically ill during the pandemic was something that helped me understand how to really make sure that my health is a priority.

A Report

Brendan Docherty

Harmony of Expressions

The most challenging journey that I have faced is my grades. During my entire life, I have always had promise, upside, and potential, but in a lot of cases have failed to cash in on it. I have had bad habits of putting things off, procrastinating, and forcing myself to make academic comebacks just to have a respectable (but not great) finish to semesters. This dates back long before college and was even a problem during high school.

I went to high school at Luke M. Powers Catholic High school, a very prestigious and well respected school here in Michigan, but that doesn't mean I was putting up a prestigious performance all the time. I have always had a bad habit of putting more time and effort into extra curriculars, this was no different during high school. I played basketball during my time, and even made all my teams early in the tryout process because of the effort I put in. But while I was thriving on the basketball court, I was struggling in the classroom and was barely pushing a 3.0. I essentially put myself in a loop of horrible starts to the semester, making a respectable comeback at the end, rinse, and repeating for 4 long years.

This put me in a nerve-racking place when applying for colleges. I got a blessing in not having to use ACT scores, but still had under a 3.0, which is not a desirable place to be when applying for higher education. Somehow, I got into all the colleges I applied to, but none of them were the school I really wanted to go to. That is, however, until I got accepted to the University of

Michigan – Flint through the formerly known Promise Scholar Program, which has been one of the biggest blessings of my life. This opened an opportunity to get used to college life a full semester early, set my GPA in a great starting place, and be energized and prepared for the Fall.

Unfortunetly, I fell back into old habits during my first fall. After and amazing summer, and coming in with a 4.0, I let myself get content and would fail classes and underachieve in the process. During this time, I was thriving in my Fraternity, taking leadership positions early and winning awards in just my freshman year, however, again, the school piece was struggling. This would continue until the Winter of 2024, in which I turned everything around. I finally found a degree that I excelled in and was able to mix my priorities successfully, that being History.

After 5 semesters of putting stuff off, underachieving, and putting myself at risk of being kicked out of not only the KCP Program, but also my Fraternity, with being on the up or out process. In my 6th semester at this University, and 7th semester in the program, I have finally overcome my habits and struggles, and have successfully attained a 3.50 semester GPA. While my accumulated GPA is still just under 3.0, I am on the fast track to, for the first time in my life, having a 3.0+ GPA.

My struggles with school have by far been one of the biggest things I've had to overcome in life, I have finally done it. This taught me very quickly that not only can you overcome even your biggest

Harmony of Expressions

struggles and set backs, but if you can find the right degree program, it can make a monumental difference for your future and your motivation.

A Poem

An Anonymous Writer

Harmony of Expressions

Calm Before the Storm

The calm before the storm

That's how it was

Middle school was the calm

High school was the storm

The storm lasted a long time

But no one ever talks about what comes next

The other side is so sublime

A little girl so vexed

Didn't see what would happen next

The calm after the storm

Living through it long enough to transform

To come out on the other side

And to have a new sense of pride

A Poem

Marah Cusac

Harmony of Expressions

washing away all the layers
of who i once was
to please everyone else
i'm done with pretending i'm someone i'm not
it's time to be me this life is all i've got
people may misunderstand me
and i've accepted that
staring at the mirror seeing my reflection
for the first time in my life i feel a connection
between my body and my mind
i finally feel alive

A Personal Essay

Drew Conner

Harmony of Expressions

Sometimes there's absolutely nothing going on in your life, so you have to live in NEET limbo for a while. This was the case for me about a year ago. I tried to find work wherever I could, but was almost comically unsuccessful. It soon dawned on me that a small but not insignificant benefit of employment was just having a place to go during the day. I figure that's the reason that an 8 hour work day for some office jobs consists of about 2-3 hours of work, with the rest dedicated to finding new and exciting ways to sort of 'perform' being busy so that no one catches on, a seemingly mandatory charade for which I blame John Calvin. See also, the rightfully reviled phrase, "If you've got time to lean, you've got time to clean."

It really did seem like I couldn't find work no matter what I did, and I really did need some. I even interviewed for the same job I'd just quit, which I was sure I'd left on good terms, but ended up getting the form rejection letter all the same. I figured that I could live with that though, at least for a little bit. I'd been going a mile a minute for my classes the past several months, so I liked that I had an opportunity to relax. I was also still mad at management there, they fired my buddy for an incident where she was completely in the right, which anyone could back up. At any rate, It looked like a good opportunity to kick my feet up.

Video games lost their spark after a short while, the reason why still escapes me. I couldn't spend all day cooking either. The only other thing that I could think of was just walking around town. So that's

Conner

what I did. As it turns out, doing that is the quickest way to confirm that the suburbs really want you dead. The urban planners threw you to the wolves 60 years ago, you had no choice in the matter, and there's no better example of this than Miller Road.

If you're going westward, once you cross Ballenger and get into Flint Township, the sidewalk just ends, returning 20 feet from the bus stop before disappearing again. When you get to the bridge over I-75, you'll find that the sidewalk is now on the opposite side of the road, at which point you either have to cross the road or start walking in the road with traffic. You could also choose option C, death, but that comes free with the other two. I ride a bike as my main form of transportation, and West Miller Road is a place that I will never go. Hell, my dad won't even go there and he can actually drive a car.

The Flint River Trail is really the only way I can get places. It used to be the old rail line that went to Chevy In The Hole, which they paved over when they must've finally realized that GM wasn't going to need freight to be taken to/from the plant anymore. It's surrounded by trees, and I actually found something in those trees. One day, while coming from work after I'd actually found a job, I noticed something that I recognized as the entrance to a clearing. It was surrounded by incredibly thick brush, and curiosity got the better of me.

The only thing in there was a fire pit, and it was a remarkably clean space. I began to spend some time there. Nobody ever asked what I meant when I'd say "I'm going to the pit." Pretty often, I'd bring with

Harmony of Expressions

me a couple beers and a pack of hot dogs, light up a fire and I would sit there cooking. The brush was so thick, it seemed to cut everything off from the outside world, making what was inside the clearing louder. I'd hear rustling in the tree line from time to time, and I'd often call out for them to join me for some drinks and food, but no one ever did.

A Personal Essay

Lanique Collins

Harmony of Expressions

Throughout the entirety of my college career, I have learned a lot about myself. I have learned to love the hustle and struggle to meet all of my goals. I started my college career in fall 2019 at Mott Community College, MCC, located here in Flint, MI. After covid-19 and a few long semesters, I finally received my associates degree in 2022. Covid-19 became very discouraging as a freshman college student. I was adjusted to going to class to understand the material. This pandemic became a pivotal moment in my life that forced me to adapt in new situations no matter the circumstance. I learned that I can overcome challenges under the pressure of everyday life and deadlines. Also during my time at MCC, I started my own business called "Nique Wink" that provides the service of eyelash extensions to anyone who wants to enhance their natural beauty.

I developed this business as just a side hustle in 2021, while trying to keep up with the pressure of college. The business started to grow and became an outlet for me to relieve stress. The thought of making someone feel even more beautiful has been very fulfilling. Through my business I have also developed severe time management skills. I have a schedule that allows me to get the most out of my day, every day. This all included attending class, working part time, running a business, having time for the gym, and studying/completing assignments.

The schedule I created during this time was easy but actually sticking to the schedule was challenging on days I wanted to just be lazy. I overcome this obstacle by reminding myself that I am watering seeds that will come to fruition when the time comes. This allowed me to work harder for my future self. While going through this schedule, I noticed that I was still feeling a certain fatigue that caused my grades to drop. That is when I learned that I need to incorporate more "me time" into my schedule during the day. This was a pivotal moment for me because it marked the beginning of me taking my mental health very seriously. I had to invest time to water my own grass before I was able to water the things in my life that I wanted to grow.

Once I graduated from MCC, I began to go after my bachelors degree at Grand Valley State University studying sport management. I chose sport management because I loved business and I love sports. I was very athletic in high school and I was the baseball manager of our varsity team. I figured it was the perfect opportunity to enhance my business skills in the sports world. Though, after one long semester at Grand Valley, I found out that the sports path was no longer for me. With this, I found my new love instead of sports, I wanted to be a marketing major. I was technically already a marketer for my own business and I love the marketing aspect in it. I learned that I admire the creativity and business side of marketing. I finished out one year at Grand Valley before I decided to move back home to Flint in 2023 to pursue my marketing degree here at the University of Michigan. I have learned so much throughout my college career, I am excited to say I will be a proud graduate from U of M in 2025.

A Poem

Kiara Colin

Harmony of Expressions

Dear flower, how have you been?
Have you seen how far you left from home Though some see this as growth,
others see it as a loath of where you came from
Despite that you're still the same as ever You never wilted or felt ashamed
You became lifted and free
It was within you that was strong
That's not wrong, dear flower
It's clear as day
Despite not being near, you still shower us with love
Above all dear flower, you're still here

A Personal Essay

Anonymous

Harmony of Expressions

I struggle with procrastination. It's been a problem in my life for as long as I can remember. I usually have the motif of "Have a lot of energy, lose that energy over the school year, start being late on assignments." This has also been extended through me having a job. This was not my laziest time though. My laziest time was during 10th grade in 2020.

It wasn't easy during high school. I was more focused because of how close I was to the finish line, but I still struggled quite a bit. I was mostly able to push through thought. This wouldn't be the case for 10th grade though as it was during the year 2020, when everything got shut down due to Covid-19. I had gotten covid during this year, but that wasn't what caused my issues. My biggest issue was dealing with online classes.

I don't do well with online classes. I look at home as my place to rest and relax, which is impossible to do when you have to do work from home. My mind still made me think that I should relax when I knew I needed to do stuff. That year gave me the most E's I've had in a year. My classes essentially went in this order of difficulty: Choir was just singing and recordings which I already liked doing, English didn't have much, Gym was easy but my laziness would still kick in, Geometry and Economics were both done through the same program so I just did them both but I wouldn't want to do them which is where most of my problems came from, Science was so confusing and I just had no interest in it so it was difficult to focus. These factors lead to the year being mostly filled with laziness and not wanting to

Harmony of Expressions

get things done. I almost failed some of these classes because of how lazy I had become when I just wanted to lay down and play games all day.

I've gotten better compared to how I originally acted in 10th grade. The next year I focused all my time and attention on school and this pushed me into my final year with 3 AP classes. I didn't do amazing with them but I felt I had shown that I can do well. High school ended great, but it sucked in the beginning. I worked hard afterwards and made it further and have tried to keep this going into college.

Covid ruined a lot of things for people. It also made things more difficult for others even during the simplest things. School became more frustrating and plenty of people lost a lot of focus. These are not excuses for how I acted and what I did during this year. I was late on many things when I shouldn't have been and didn't want to do anything even when I knew I needed to. I've gotten better about this and that year will remain in my mind. If I keep thinking about it, then I should never lose my focus and remember to do what is needed.

Eternal Bonds: Siblings United in Love and Lost

Kenyatta Choice

Harmony of Expressions

In the depths of my sorrow, I found strength,
Bound by love and memories, I go to any length.
My brother's light, forever shining bright,
Guiding us though the darkest night.

His laughter echoes in my heart,
A bond unbreakable, though we're apart.
My dreams ignited, by his spark which left a mark on me.

Through tears and pain, I rise anew,
His spirit within us, strong and true.
We carry his legacy, a flame that won't fade,
In his honor, we'll never be swayed.

I face each day with unwavering might,
Determined to make their spirit take flight.
With resilience as our shield, I stand tall,
For my brother's dreams, I give it my all.

Through it all, I stand side by side,
With strength and love, I won't hide.
In honor of my brother, I'll make him proud.
With every step I take his spirit soars,
In my heart, his memory forever adores.
I'll chase my dream never looking back,
For my brother's legacy, I'll stay on track.

In his absence, I'll carry the flame,
For my brother's sake, I'll conquer and claim.
With resilience as I shield, I stand tall,
For my brother, I'll give it my all and more.

Porcelain

Aniya Loren Callaway

Harmony of Expressions

Callaway

I am made of porcelain,
Fragile, breaking down,
My emotions have fled,
Leaving me empty and numb.

A mask hides my sorrow,
Concealing the cracks within,
Shielding my loneliness,
Afraid to let anyone in.

I am made of porcelain,
This mask wears me thin,
Tired, weak, and shattered,
My spirit breaking from within.

"Smile for the camera!"
Does this happiness deceive?
Am I dancing through delight,
Or is joy just make-believe?

I am made of porcelain,
Begging for repair,
Broken and falling apart,
A burden too much to bear.

Let the mask come off,
Reveal the truth beneath,
Grant me solace and peace,
Release me from this grief.

I am made of porcelain.

A Poem

Anonymous Writer

Harmony of Expressions

In a world of wonder, a bond's decree,
Hearts entwined in love's silent plea.
From distant shores or lands nearby,
A family formed under the same sky.

In tender arms, a new journey begins,
Where hope ignites and pasts rescind.
In the embrace of love's pure art,
A child finds home, a brand new start.

Through trials faced and victories won,
In each other's love, they find the sun.
For in adoption's embrace, we see,
The beauty of love's boundless decree.

A Personal Essay

Alexander Brown

Harmony of Expressions

In a matter of a single year, a lot of things changed for better or for worse going forward. In the year 2020 the world was put to a halt, the whole world was locked inside all because of a pandemic, a pandemic caused by Covid-19. It was a big setback for a lot of individuals as well as business, a setback many still are trying to recover from to this day. For me, just like others, Covid-19 was a hurdle getting over and the effects of it still linger for me.

When the pandemic first began; I believe in the middle of march, I was in the final stretch of my junior year. Everything was going so smoothly, my grades were good and life was good. During this time I was taking a medical course and we were a week away from our clinical trip where we get to get experience in a hospital, the trip I worked really hard to get to that whole semester. Then boom It's canceled because of the rise of a virus spreading around, a couple days later schools are closed next. Clinicals are canceled and school is out and now I'm sitting in the house enjoying the little break from school but completely oblivious to what's to come. See in my head I'm thinking "oh it's gonna blow over in a week", but was I wrong. Not long after the school closings the government issued a nationwide lockdown, halting everyone in their tracks.

Covid changed a lot of things going forward. I feel like after covid the world became a lot more distant, especially for me. During my isolation I forgot how to socialize like I used to, I forgot how to interact with others, I felt alone. And then came my senior year, an important year for me as a high school student. Because of covid my senior year was stolen from me, our classes were completely online and soulless. Looking back it's hard to say I even had a real senior year, it felt like I was hardly there. Eventually our school did return to in-person classes but from what I hear it still wasn't the same. I didn't get to go back to normal classes because I was impaired at the time, causing me to continue online classes. Even though the classes were back to in-person, it still had its setbacks, the students still had to do classes via laptops and isolate between students, it kept us safe of course but it was still completely soulless.

This was such a stressful point in my life and soon it was the time to prepare for college, Covid was such a setback for me it slipped my mind that I was even a senior at the time. Even with all the problems I still made it though, I graduated and I applied for colleges eventually ending up at UofM flint. Unfortunately I was almost gatekept by Covid again. Because of Covid, a lot of schools required a full vaccine before attending and they would refuse you if you could not get one. This was a problem for me because I wasn't vaccinated at the time, and for certain reasons I wasn't planning on getting it either. Eventually things got settled and I was accepted into UofM flint, but had Covid-19 not existed prior there would have been no problems with my entry.

Looking back on the last four years, it's been pretty rough. I've had to deal with many ups and downs in my life, some of them are from Covid and some from others. But the point of it all is I never

Harmony of Expressions

gave up, I never let anything stop me from getting to this point and that's exactly why Im here today writing this essay. I'm thankful for every experience in my life and I'm thankful that I made it this far in life and I plan to keep on trucking until the wheels fall off.

A Personal Essay

Joseph Bishai

Harmony of Expressions

The Covid-19 pandemic brought with it unprecedented challenges, disrupting lives and upending plans in its wake. As I reflect on the past year, I am reminded of the resilience and determination it took to navigate through such uncertain times, all while striving towards my goal of college acceptance.

When the pandemic hit, it felt like the world had come to a standstill. Schools closed, gatherings were prohibited, and life as we knew it was put on hold. Suddenly, the future seemed more uncertain than ever before. Like many others, I found myself grappling with feelings of anxiety and fear, unsure of what the future held.

But amidst the chaos, there was a glimmer of hope. Despite the challenges posed by Covid-19, I remained steadfast in my determination to pursue higher education. For me, getting accepted into college was more than just a goal—it was a lifeline, a symbol of hope and opportunity in the face of adversity.

The college application process was daunting, to say the least. With the world in turmoil and the future uncertain, it was easy to feel overwhelmed. But I refused to let fear hold me back. I poured my heart and soul into my applications, determined to make the most of this opportunity despite the challenges that lay ahead.

As the acceptance letters began to roll in, each one felt like a small victory—a testament to my perseverance and determination in the face of adversity. But it was the moment I received my acceptance letter from my top-choice college that truly changed everything.

The feeling of relief and joy that washed over me was indescribable. In that moment, all the hard work and sacrifices I had made felt worth it. Getting accepted into college wasn't just a validation of my academic achievements—it was a symbol of hope, a beacon of light in an otherwise dark and uncertain time.

But my journey didn't end there. As I prepared to embark on this new chapter of my life, the reality of the ongoing pandemic loomed large. Covid-19 continued to pose challenges and obstacles, forcing me to adapt and overcome in ways I never imagined. But through it all, I remained resilient. I refused to let fear and uncertainty dictate my future. Instead, I focused on what I could control, embracing each challenge as an opportunity for growth and learning. As I look back on the past year, I am filled with a sense of pride and gratitude. Despite the hardships and obstacles I faced, I never lost sight of my goals. And now, as I prepare to embark on this new chapter of my life, I do so with a renewed sense of purpose and determination.

The journey through Covid and college acceptance has been one of the most challenging experiences of my life. But it has also been one of the most rewarding. It has taught me the importance of resilience, perseverance, and the power of hope in the face of adversity.

As I look towards the future, I do so with optimism and excitement. I know that the road ahead

Harmony of Expressions

will be filled with challenges and obstacles, but I also know that I have the strength and determination to overcome them. And for that, I am eternally grateful.

A Personal Essay

Kayley Christian

Harmony of Expressions

I almost gave up singing, on several occasions. After I entered college, and while I was doing my degree. I'm still a year out from graduating from the University of Michigan-Flint and I am thoroughly satisfied with the work that I have done to achieve this level of satisfaction with everything. However, this semester of Winter 2024 I was under a lot of stress and pressure. As a music performance major, we have to take technical classes like the music educators just not as many as them. Fundamentals, Theory, History, Harmony, and Technology. These are things that should be given to beginners. I did not understand this when I first entered college, theory especially was difficult for me. Being analytical is not my strongest trait, I am a person that likes to feel and express answers with my emotions and while I understand being analytical it's hard to explain it back to someone. The stress of the semester hit me hard, on top of being analytical, I had to retake a class that I needed a higher grade in, and the bowling ball sized cherry on top, was my Senior Recital which was in very high anticipation. Practicing almost everyday, memorizing eight German Lied (German Art Song) song cycle, perfecting a duet that I played with my special person, and acting out for arias (Opera Solos) and Cabaret pieces.

    While all of this pressure and burn out stress was on my shoulders, I began to really think… "Is this actually worth it? Is this going to be the rest of my life? Do I want to continue singing?" While driving with my duet partner, she asked me "Are you okay?". I burst into tears at that moment and I told

Christian

her no. I explained everything that I was feeling and going through. I hated what I was feeling and I was actually scared. My life had been surrounded by all kinds of music since I was a kid, and classical music wrapped me together when I entered high school. Now as a 23 year old woman, I was feeling like music was hurting me more than making me feel happy like it normally did. I didn't want to hate the one concept that gave me a push to do better in my lifetime. When we arrived home, we came up with a plan. She, our other flatmate and I agreed that I was burnt out. We are all music students and burnout happens a lot for us. I was told by my partner to take the next day off. It was a Wednesday evening and the next day was another practice day with my vocal teacher. I had to email her and my choral director that I would not be there, as well as my keyboard professor. My accompanist was worried about me. He and I had become friends at that point, spending several years making music together. I consider this man as a trusted friend. He had obtained his masters as well as my other professors. I emailed all of them, asking for the same thing. "What made you keep going when, when you wanted to just quit." While I got good answers, I still had a lot to do.

The semester has finally finished, and I am proud of everything I have accomplished and now, I'm still questioning myself, and taking a break from singing. But I found my love for music and my passion for classical music again. I am proud to be a musician, a vocalist, and an artist.

A Poem

Arianna Barginere-Claxton

Harmony of Expressions

dear future self,
you're welcome.
everything that i sacrifice now
I know it'll all be worth it in the end. I'm here making you proud and i pray you I never think I failed.
Every day, every moment, every second I try. i try to continue for you so you can look back and maybe thank me one day. i'm sorry for all of the bad choices i make But I'm still learning.
I'm sorry i just don't know as well as you do but i promise to give you good memories to look back on
so you can say
"i made it" or "i did it"
I promise to never give up on you.

A Poem

Timothy Baird

Harmony of Expressions

In the midst of masks and empty halls, my senior year did unfold,
No grand procession, no stories told.
Yet amidst the silence, a quiet strength did grow,
First-generation dreams, determination to show.
Though denied the stage, the applause, the cheer,
I found solace in the journey, not just the destination near.
With every hurdle, every setback faced,
A resolve emerged, firmly placed.
For while the world grappled with uncertainty's glare,
I focused on the future, beyond this affair.
Through screens and solitude, I forged ahead,
With hope as my compass, no fear to tread.
In the absence of ceremony's grand decree,
I embraced the challenge, I dared to be free.
For in the heart of adversity, I found my voice,
A testament to resilience, my ultimate choice.
So let the absence of pomp not define my fate,
For the essence of achievement transcends any date.
In the quiet triumphs, the struggles overcome,
Lies the true graduation, where dreams are won.

A Creative Visual

Harmony of Expressions

College isn't a race. Take your time and go at your own pace. Because it's never too late to succeed.

Lessons In Transitions

Mekka Al-Shawi

Harmony of Expressions

To me, college has been a home for many lessons, of course, not just the ones I learned during my classes but also the ones I got to live. Like learning from the people I met, made friends with, and learned to love. But also the hardships I faced and the revolutions I experienced as a person, through my mental, gender, and sexual orientation. Along with unpacking personal traumas I encountered and deconstructed.

If you met me during my freshman year you would not have met Mekka, but instead, someone who presented as a bit more masculine, was very insecure and truly didn't see a place for herself in life. She didn't understand herself but thought she somehow knew how the world worked when she didn't even let herself see it. She let other people, namely her mother, define the life she lived.

As a child, I was called quiet and shy by teachers who used that as a compliment compared to other kids. However, I wasn't quiet just to behave well, but because I was so afraid of disappointing people, my teachers, and especially my mother. My mother kept and still holds very high standards for me, standards that restricted me for so much of my life and led to me living just to make her happy instead of finding ways to make me happy. I cast aside interests that she didn't want me to express, ones that might have shown I wasn't straight or cisgender like playing with women's clothes, makeup, or girl's toys. A boy doing those things would be made fun of and she wanted to prevent that but also had her homophobic reasons for repressing me.

As I was packing and getting ready to move into my dorm, that's when it hit me that who I was at home did not need to be who I was at this entirely new school in a whole new city. No one in Flint would know me or even care, this was a time to change everything about me and find that joy I held myself away from.

My first goal was to find safe spaces on campus, the Intercultural Center (ICC) and the Center of Gender and Sexuality (CGS) being the main ones. At CGS I could finally explore my sexuality and later on, gender as I shifted to identifying as nonbinary after their Coming Out Monologues event resonated with me. I never felt comfortable calling myself a boy or being seen as one and wanted to recontextualize the identity I existed in.

At the ICC I could explore my racial identity, I never got the chance to be around other Black people aside from my family before, especially ones that reflected a lot of my personal views and even being queer themselves. At one of their events, a new member of CAPS (Counseling and Psychological Services) was introducing themself and I used that as a chance to get started with CAPS services and started therapy marking yet another journey for myself.

Of course, some missteps were taken when getting my bearings in these spaces, and lashed out at people I judged too quickly and tried to take control of spaces I just entered as new things scared me, even if those new things could be good.
So even if I was experiencing finally getting to

Harmony of Expressions

express myself as queer and nonbinary, so many things still felt wrong. I still felt very alone, especially in my own dorm. I just couldn't relate or get along with my white male roommates and dreaded even going back to my room after classes. This stress of not feeling comfortable where I sleep and losing control of who I thought it was led to multiple breakdowns, a change of dorm rooms, and a new roommate.

From the first day meeting my new roommate I felt an instant connection, that this could be someone I could get close to and can understand me. This new friendship turned into what I thought was romance, never having a relationship before. But, for the first time in my life, I felt so happy not just being with someone but with new friendships and letting myself dress differently and present myself as a new joyous person who wanted to explore the world. That didn't last long though as the semester and the school year ended with me back home for the summer where I returned to being the boy I was when I left.

However, I still had my new friends to talk to, mostly my roommate. Similar to me, she was experiencing major changes herself as she started her transition as a transgender woman and began Hormone Replacement Therapy (HRT). Around this time I started to hate her and got so bitter. I didn't understand why or even thought it was healthy, but I hated hearing about the changes she was making, getting to start this major journey, and even exploring the country at that time. I hated that she got to experience so much and was afraid of her changing into someone I didn't recognize until I realized I was jealous and wanted the same for me.

That summer was when I realized I was a woman. Coming back to school with her returning as my roommate enabled me to start the same journey she did. She sat in with me as I made the call to schedule an appointment for me to start HRT and even walked me over to show me how to get to the clinic when the day came. Even though our exact relationship had changed she was still one of my closest friends and someone I knew I could rely on.

The appointment itself was quick and everything seemed to just click for me, as that same day I got my medicine. And taking it that day was one of the easiest decisions I ever made, for once in my life I didn't feel anxiety or that something bad would happen. Instead, I knew that this meant that I would be so much happier than I was before. And every day I think back and see how right I was.

As of writing this, I'm well over a year on HRT, and around the same time as starting it, I also renamed myself Mekka. A name reflective of my heritage but also one that truly sparked joy whenever I heard others say it and also when I said it to myself. And finding things like that, things that I choose for myself and make me happy became my most important goal.

Instead of living for others, I chose to live how I see fit. I cannot allow myself to be deeply impacted by others who judge me when I know they come from a place of ignorance or hate or - like how I

Harmony of Expressions

used to - try to get others to conform to the standards they're used to. I've been called a freak, devil worshipper, faggot, and other names and of course, they hurt me when I heard them initially but also showed me how insecure people are. To try and tear me down when I just want to live my life openly as I see fit. I love to dress however I want in different styles seeing what clothes go with what and people recognize the joy I have and shower me with compliments. I recently won an award for inclusive leadership through the work I do on campus and walked across a stage in front of a room full of people in a dress that I never thought I would get to wear. The euphoria I felt was unlike anything I experienced before. These moments I cherish and know that this is exactly who I am meant to be.

    I'm glad to be able to say that I am Mekka Al-Shawi, a Black Iraqi transgender woman who lives to make herself happy. I also strive to educate others and create safe spaces for those like me when I first came to the UM-Flint campus through my current work at the ICC in collaboration with CGS called Queerness in Color. All of these combine to create a full circle moment for me, in that I get to work for spaces where I felt safest and get to be that representation and voice that I didn't have for myself years ago.

A Personal Essay

Anonymous

Harmony of Expressions

How can anyone plan how their lives are going to pan out. Here is the truth, you can't. No one knows where the road to success leads or even if the road will ever lead to success. One thing is for certain. The most important thing is not the destination, but the moments and lessons taught along the way.

I initially wanted to do cyber security as a profession when I left high school. Now I want to focus on a career that helps people face-to-face. During my first year of college, I made some pretty great friendships. I had never experienced such an engaging interaction with others as I had this year. I always wonder what it would have been like if I did not reach out to my roommate if he needed a roommate himself. The butterfly effect is an interesting topic of discussion because we can never really predict what may happen based on little events. It is also like the domino effect. An event as little as saying hello to a stranger may completely alter the trajectory of one's path in life, for better or worse.

Without the help of my friends, I can't say how I would have performed academically this year. I find it very important to keep someone to hold you accountable for academics, work, and other reasons. My friends made sure that I stayed on task and was focused on what was important. As for now, I am attending classes over the summer while I assist my mother at taking care of my six younger siblings.

College has taught me a lot about holding myself accountable while managing multiple other responsibilities. I have worked two jobs all while attending classes which has molded my brain into an academic machine. The art of juggling tasks is a skill that is valuable in today's world. Not everyone can handle taking on as many responsibilities as I had this semester. I am not trying to

Harmony of Expressions

boast but I'd say I did well. I had never done anything like this, especially during high school. I was a below average student who had very little aspirations. I did not know what my calling was and to this day I still don't know exactly what I am called to do. What I am sure of though is that I want to help others and I enjoy the grind of taking care of responsibilities. There are some jobs that I prefer over others but overall, I feel like this first year has taught me to appreciate the grind as it is a reward to work towards a goal as important as obtaining a degree. I also have my friends and family here to cheer me on as I am striving to succeed which is a blessing that I cannot express more gratitude for. As long as I am breathing, I will continue to pursue my goals without ever slowing down. Though the future is uncertain, with the mentality that I have, I feel like nothing is impossible.

Made in the USA
Monee, IL
05 March 2025